WINNING WITH IP

MANAGING INTELLECTUAL PROPERTY TODAY

INSPIRING HIGH GROWTH AND
CAPTURING BREAK-OUT VALUE

Managing Intellectual Property Today:
Inspiring high growth and capturing break-out value

Every possible effort has been made to ensure that the information contained in this publication is accurate at the time of going to press. Neither the publisher nor the authors can accept responsibility for any errors or omissions, however caused. Nor can any responsibility be accepted for loss or damage as a result of reading this publication.

Fifth edition published for Newsdesk Global Communications by Novaro Publishing
e: publish@novaropublishing.com.

ISBN: 978-1-0685644-1-3

A CIP catalogue record for this book is available from the British Library.

Designed by Chantel Barnett, Clear Design CC Ltd

For further details about our titles and our authors, see:
novaropublishing.com and winningwithip.com

WINNING WITH IP

MANAGING INTELLECTUAL PROPERTY TODAY

INSPIRING HIGH GROWTH AND
CAPTURING BREAK-OUT VALUE

CONSULTANT EDITOR

ADAM JOLLY

Newsdesk Global
Independent Book Publishers

NOVARO
PUBLISHING

CONTENTS

FOREWORD

The intellectual property in Europe's deep tech is now being mobilised to upgrade its capacity to create value at the same level as the United States and China. Historically, Europe has fallen behind in innovation, even though it has remained a research superpower. Now it is accepting the challenge to catch the next wave of technologies and bring them to market.

The European Innovation Council, a €10 billion programme of the European Union established in 2021, has been supporting breakthrough technologies and start-ups in deep tech with the capacity to scale. In its first three years, it supported over 500 start-ups, 275 advanced research programmes and 140 commercialisation projects. In the process, the EIC has now become Europe's largest investor in early-stage deep-tech ventures and is making an impact on the scaling of European companies, having supported over 150 centaurs (valuations above €100 million), out of which 15 have a valuation above €500 million including eight over €1 billion (Impact Report, EIC, 2023).

In our programmes at the EIC, IP has a fundamental role to play in the whole cycle of identifying, testing, launching and scaling ideas that are high risk, but have the potential to become gamechangers for our economy or society. For us IP is not a matter of ticking boxes. We are supporting projects to protect IP and encouraging ventures to file patents as part of a well-thought-out IP strategy in support of their business goals.

At the start, in our early-stage projects, such as Pathfinder, we want researchers to think about the competitive landscape in which they operate and the IP they could create, not just for the sake of filing a patent (as important as it may be), but as the foundation of a possible exploitation strategy. It can be eye opening when you investigate the space around your technology and see who else is playing in the same space. It will help you to identify your market and build your IP portfolio around it.

With partners, such as the European Patent Office, we can analyse the inventive merit and the proposed future IP strategy of the proposals (as per EIC WP 2025). In 2024, out of the 81 proposals who were invited to the jury phase of the evaluation, 19 had no patent yet, 40 had applications pending and 22 had patent protection. Of the 40 selected for funding, 36 had good prospects for patentability and 31 had promising patents of their own, which indicates the importance of IP, while showing that having a patent is not a goal in itself.

Further on, in Transition projects which invest up to €2.5 million into further maturation of a breakthrough technology and its business plan, we expect a clear sense of how the IP is going to be further developed and monetised. Here we recognise that there is not a one size fits all as you go towards the market. Researchers and project members can embrace different roles from more technical to more entrepreneurial and we build the programme around them. What is important is that the results of a promising project do not remain in the lab while our competitors move resolutely towards the market.

Many projects or ventures don't take account of different routes to market: many overlook licensing as an option and miss out the additional revenue streams it can create. Of course, this route needs to make sense in the overall IP and business strategy.

For candidates looking to scale with the EIC Accelerator programme, which awards up to €2.5 million in grant and coinvests up to €10 million in equity, we expect not just the IP rights to be securely in place, but an active strategy to manage them. It's proving a worthwhile question to ask. For every euro we invest, we crowd in private capital that contributes between three and five times as much.

Within this chain of value that IP inspires, we can't expect everyone to get it all right. The passage of a technology's readiness level from its creation (at TRL 1) to being ready for market (at TRL 9) is long and complicated. At the start, in particular, it can be difficult to imagine that the IP could eventually have a huge value.

As part of our programmes, we run a series of support services for our deep-tech beneficiaries at each stage of their development, whether it is coaching, which can guide our projects through different stages of technology commercialisation, or training, business model exploration or even venture building. These support services can bring the next venture up to speed and increase the chances of success in a competitive landscape.

For our programmes, we are equally happy for projects or their spin-offs to draw on local support, whether from local accelerators or a university's technology transfer office. It's also why we are delighted to contribute to this book which gives founders and innovators a vivid and practical sense of the role that IP in all its forms is now playing in inspiring high growth and capturing value.

In Europe, where only one third of patents are commercialised (Competitiveness Compass, EU, 2025), prospects for high-growth tech remain far from perfect, of course. By number of start-ups or spin-offs, Europe might be catching up with the US, but the scaling up is where the issue is. European venture capitalists are smaller in size, attract less capital than their US counterparts and are limited by scale-up capital. Our goal is to create a strong financial ecosystem in which startups and spin-offs can thrive and, at the EIC, we are now doing more to support the scale-up phase by making higher investments, ie, between €10 million and €30 million (STEP, scale-up scheme, EIC).

In Europe, we all might be having our doubts about our future prospects and what our priorities should be. We can, at least, be confident that our research will continue to be amongst the best in the world. To restore our prosperity, however, we must keep learning how to identify and develop IP with the power to transform our economy, so we are amongst the leaders of the next wave of disruptive technologies.

Viorel Peca,
Head of Transition,
European Innovation Council

- *The views expressed in this article are the responsibility of the author and do not necessarily reflect the views of the European Patent Office, European Commission nor of the European Innovation Council and SMEs Executive Agency. These organisations are not liable for any consequence stemming from the reuse of this article.*

1

FUTURE INDUSTRY GIANTS

The billions of dollars in new value that digital is creating will predominantly flow to those who best manage their intellectual assets. The winners could come from anywhere, says Audrey Yap at the High-growth Technology Business Initiative

If we look at previous industrial revolutions, whether mass production or automation, it was those who used their intellectual property to monetise their technology who emerged as the giants of their time. It's the same today. Enormous value is being created as we switch to digital.

Just consider a typical oil rig as an example. It has 80,000 sensors, generating data on parameters, temperature, flow and equipment. In total, it amounts to two terabytes of data a day, well beyond the bounds of conventional analysis, which is why it relies on advances in artificial intelligence and machine learning to start capturing its potential.

It is a pattern that it is being repeated everywhere. By connecting sensors, a complete data picture of the manufacturing process emerges that will transform how decisions are made. Five years ago, 10 percent of manufacturers were close to implementing this industrial internet of things. Now it's moving rapidly beyond 50 percent.

This new infrastructure is creating the foundation for new applications and future growth. Smart factories are transforming operations. Predictive analytics is limiting the $50 billion that downtime costs manufacturers each year. Digital twins, which either simulate a device or an entire process, are being widely applied, ultimately saving as much $1 trillion for manufacturers. Such advances are driving growth in the adoption of the 5G standard for transferring high volumes of data at speed and for exploring AI-based solutions.

The billions of dollars in new value that are being created will predominantly flow to those who best manage their intellectual assets (IAs) to underpin their technology innovations. Anyone can win. Their identity will depend largely on whether they can establish exclusivity of use and a dominant design. As well as selling more products at a higher margin, they can leverage their portfolios to broaden their funding options with techniques like IP securitisation and IP loans. In turn, IAs open up strategic pathways like licensing and collaboration as an alternative to equity and the dilution of shareholdings. On the other side of the equation, a more active market is being created in the acquisition of tech ventures and their underlying IAs, which will establish a more widely recognised benchmark for future valuations.

So let us review how the future value in IAs is likely to be won. What are the strategies that today's giants are pursuing? To what extent can IAs act as an equaliser for smaller tech ventures allowing them to establish their own degree of dominance? How are tech ventures globally deploying their IAs to establish an advantage? And what are some of the principles we can draw in how IP is being managed to become a tech giant of tomorrow?

Today's giants

At ZTE, the Chinese telecoms giant, revenues are generated from IAs in two ways: directly and indirectly. In total, it has a portfolio of 80,000 patents and invests 10 percent of its annual revenues in IP and innovation.

Directly, it supplies technology to the main telecoms' carriers through standards in co-operation with its competitors in a way that ensures that everyone makes a fair return. Once you are in this position, explains Marco Tong, ZTE's deputy head of IP, it becomes possible to cross-license technologies, so keeping the peace between everyone and letting each of them focus on their own business.

At the same time, you can take a more indirect approach to maximising the value of your IAs. In ZTE's case, it might mean forming joints ventures using IAs as equity or by authorising start-ups to use its technology, which represents a way for ZTE to enter new industries or open up different markets. Alternatively, Tong says, you can use your IAs as collateral or raise money through investors who are willing to fund litigation to enhance the value of an IA.

IAs as an equaliser

Against the scale and sophistication of such an operation, what hope is there for smaller tech ventures? If they are going to move up the value chain, they can't just treat IAs as a costly afterthought or a legal nuisance. Instead, if they think like ZTE and make IAs a strategic priority, they have an equal chance, even it is on a smaller scale, to dominate a space by being clear from the start about what makes them different and how they access their technology.

It's not just about being ready to fight. What really matters is that you give yourself the leverage to slow competitors and negotiate deals that monetise the assets that you are creating. When business models now evolve in months when previously they took years to establish, tech ventures can put themselves at an advantage by being nimble enough to position themselves at the cutting edge, where they may well find themselves becoming a target for acquisitions.

Tomorrow's giants

When it comes to a deal or a funding rounding, IAs are, of course, going to be sharply defined. But what is the mindset that leads to this point. After all, at the start it's always a struggle to establish an idea, identify the right use, gain traction in the market and keep everyone in the ecosystem happy. So, let's take four early-stage examples of where value is being created: by making IP a core function, by co-sharing innovation, by competitive positioning and by managing IAs holistically.

IP as a core function

At Qualcomm's incubator, it became clear that one of the most dynamic variables for start-ups and spin-offs is how attuned they were to IP. Some founders, usually with corporate experience, are already IP savvy. For most, it's an afterthought. Even when they do address it, their implementation lets them down. So, the first question is whether a chief executive is transmitting a belief in IP as a priority. What then makes the difference is if you introduce a quarterly review of your portfolio, not just to identify what is there, but assess its potential for being monetised.

Co-sharing innovation

Before you reach the point of launching a deep tech venture, it's likely to have already consumed significant funding, research and resources. So how as a relative newcomer do you bridge this gap and manage the risks? Not by operating in isolation. At a Thai university venture builder, Visup, which has launched three spin-offs since 2020, the approach is to use IP as the basis for early-stage collaboration.

First, you identify who is working in your field, then you make a proposal how you could multiply the value of their technology, before agreeing to eventually spin off a joint venture together. By bringing in someone's existing technologies and branding, you can accelerate the research and, in this case, start talking to the Japanese market. Alternatively, you can cross-license with other spin-offs with a view to extending and co-owning the IP. At each stage of these ventures, it's IP that governs that the sharing of the innovation risks and establishes the foundation for realising its potential as spin-off or licence.

Competitive positioning

For venture capitalists, the one response at a pitch that they don't want to hear is that a technology has no competition, says the head of innovation at the London School of Economics, David Ai. We are too advanced, they say, no one else has thought of it.

Actually, there are always competitors. Existing solutions may not work as well, but are already in use. Once you do establish yourself and prove money can be made, the question is then how will you respond when other potential competitors arrive to take over your market?

You will only keep these customers, says Ai, if you have a real sense of who they are and what your appeal is. Distinguish between purchasers who care about productivity and users who are concerned with their experience. The value lies in designing a unique proposition for them all.

Holistic thinking

If deep tech, by definition, is too risky for even the earliest stage investors, then what structure can you adopt to overcome the two great bugbears that a venture will face: funding and talent? At SG Innovate, the goal is to translate cutting edge technologies into strong IP and a unique proposition. Its venture capital is dynamically intertwined with two other units: talent and community.

With talent, it develops the capabilities of graduates and executives, ready to drop into a venture. At community, it runs a broad network for those it can involve in ventures as investors, employees, ventures or manufacturers. Such a holistic approach best suits the particular challenges of bringing deep tech to life, says Lim Jui in Singapore, where SG Innovate acts as the lead agency for commercialising the next generation of technologies.

IA portfolios

When IAs are defined so holistically, it broadens their scope to anything that is novel or original: products, processes, software, data, text, appearances, formulations or manufacture. Together they fall under two broad categories.

First, you can register them in different territories as patents, designs or trade marks. Second, you can set up a process to keep them proprietary as copyright, know-how or as a trade secret.

As a future giant, you will accept that how you combine these IP rights is a high-level strategic decision. You won't delay as they are core to your prospects for realising future value. Particularly in the early stages, these IAs are your most tangible asset, which will inform your discussions with potential investors and partners, as well as determining the models you adopt to scale up your innovations.

Audrey Yap was instrumental in founding the High-growth technology business initiative, which was established by the EPO and Licensing Executives Society International to foster a strategic approach to IP among business decision-makers, train their IP professionals in business-focused IP management practices and support investors in enhancing their knowledge of IP strategy. More details at epo.org/high-technology-businesses or at HTB community on LinkedIn.

She is co-founder and managing director of Asean IP and Yusarn Audrey, a corporate practice in Singapore. She has extensive experience working with companies at various stages of growth and has been ranked one of the world's leading IP strategists in the IAM300 for 15 years. She is a past president of LESI, the global network for licensing professionals, and chairs the Singapore Innovation and Productivity Institute.

Marco Tong, deputy head of IP, ZTE, Lim Jui, chief executive, SG Innovate and **Henang Shah**, engineering lead at Qualcomm Technology Licensing, India were speaking at the High Growth Technology Business Conference, Asia, 2021. **David Ai**, head of innovation, London School of Economics and **Apiwat Thongprasert**, managing director, Visup were speaking at the High Growth Technology Business Conference, global perspectives, 2024. The full presentations are available to view at: epo.org/en/news-events/events.

2

STRATEGICALLY OPEN

Digital is making all innovation inevitably open to some degree, says Professor Bowman Heiden: the question is how to capture new value by lining up the underlying intellectual assets in the right business model

The tempo of innovation has changed. Not just for digitals but for everyone. Products that once took years to develop now go viral in months. The window of profitability has become correspondingly shorter and more intense. Fall behind the curve and you will struggle to make much of a return.

As well as being faster to market, products are becoming a combination of multiple technologies, so we are all inevitably innovating openly to some degree, whether we fully realise it or not. Take artificial intelligence. It is all about building on advances by others to develop your own version or application. As yet, no one is wholly clear about who the winners will be, although it's sure to be those who are flexible enough to combine a degree of openness with a business model that captures the value of the underlying IP.

This degree of openness can vary as we have seen with mobile standards. Google's Android is free to use with the aim of growing an ecosystem of innovations that rely on it. Apple has taken a more proprietary approach that wraps the software into the overall customer experience. Both took a view on how open they were going to be between permissive and restrictive, then built their business around it.

It's a familiar digital pattern, which is now repeating itself in other industries. In automotive, the battle is about who will own the driverless experience. Will it be the established makers? Or will they be usurped by the digital giants who have much wider experience of designing these interfaces? Or will it be a completely new set of ventures, as is often the case when industries transform? They are the ones who can leave behind legacy systems and invent for the next disruptive phase. The outcomes are still far from certain.

For automakers and their supply chains, the first step is to stop thinking of themselves as just mechanical engineers, but as suppliers of mobility. To innovate, they are going to reach beyond their own domain to bring in new technologies and solutions. Those who navigate the transition will have learnt to co-invent with new types of partner, sharing their intellectual assets within a model that allows them to compete.

For many, particularly those in the supply chain, it is a daunting prospect. Many despair of ever making a return from innovation: aren't the odds stacked against them? won't the digital tide sweep them away?

Such angst is only a first reaction. Acceptance will eventually come. A path forward can then be found that depends on becoming strategically open. It's on that basis that Philips co-created the Senseo coffee maker. As a company, it was just the kind of established hardware manufacturer that you might expect to struggle with multi-technology, convergent products. Instead, it forged an alliance with Sara Lee to redefine how we can drink coffee at home. It proved an inspired combination. It was equally creative in how it brought together two distinct cultures with diverging expectations for realising value. Philips is now applying what it learnt to forge a new partnership with ABS for how we drink beer at home.

So what does it take to reset the dial and start becoming strategically open? First, understand where you are competitively positioned. Next define your IP as digital assets. Then master the complimentary domains of open data, open source and open standards. Like Philips, you will now have the flexibility to experiment with different business models in a way that secures your intellectual assets and allows you to make a return.

No two answers will be the same. Open is a spectrum between permissive and restrictive. It is up to you to find a balance that gives you the speed and scope to explore new possibilities, setting it against the intellectual assets that give you the control to regulate the outcome in a way that favours you.

Set the dial

Digital demands that you compete and collaborate on new terms. Often you will find yourself dealing with those from outside your normal sphere. You can't assume that they will instinctively appreciate how your industry or your market works. They may well have ideas about doing it differently anyway. So before you start, ask yourself three questions about where you really stand.

First, second or third mover?

Technologies such as AI have their roots within an open culture, progressively building on one innovation after another. As a first mover, you might be looking to encourage adoption. As a third mover, you will probably prefer to build on what is freely available and establish your own distinctive point of value.

Development or distribution?

Strategic openness happens in two distinct phases. First, when you accelerate innovation by pooling resources, expertise and ideas, while guarding the ownership and usage of the results that matter to you. Second, you may chose to open access to your technology to encourage adoption or build an ecosystem around it. No uniformity governs such releases. Terms vary between going into the public domain without restriction and requirements to report back any improvements.

Contributor or beneficiary?

Within the layers of your openly sourced innovation, you want to be clear about your status as a contributor or beneficiary. If software is free to use, it's worth drawing a line with what is proprietary to you.

Typically, you will give away a free version, then offer an upgrade by paying for the full functionality.

Intellectual assets

Tech ventures tend to take a narrow view of assets within their portfolio. They often feel it's diffuse or like a cloud. Instead, it's a matter of taking a step back and thinking what could find a place within a business model. Data, observations and correlations all have value. Likewise, workarounds, visualisations, instructions and software. Typically, between 10 and 40 assets could qualify when answering the question of what is valuable, unique or within your control.

Future control points

For tomorrow's technology leaders, IP management takes on a proactive role, shaping what research to pursue and what technology to acquire. The goal is not just to protect what ideas you develop. It is to create future control points in the market. It is still relatively unusual for strategy and IP to combine in this way, even if it holds the potential to anticipate where profitability will peak.

Fill the gaps

Once strategy and IP are aligned, it becomes possible to anticipate how you might be competing in five years and what gaps you have to fill. It's an expansive question. Think widely with your collaborators about what technologies and solutions you might want to acquire. If you can line up these external sources of innovation, it will give you more scope to manage the convergence, complexity and speed that today's markets demand.

Keeping track

As you progress, it's easy to lose track of what you're bringing in and what you already have. It's a frequent sticking point when negotiating deals or exits. Instead, if you keep an inventory as you go, you will add depth to your portfolio. Otherwise, if you're put on the spot at short notice about what clearances you have for being open, it can be awkward to fix.

Digital assets

Those developing smart products are inevitably being drawn into innovating openly, as they rely to different degrees on open data, open source and open standards to facilitate their adoption of new technologies such as AI and machine learning. Each has its distinct characteristics, so it is easy to treat them as separate domains. The challenge is to combine their varying degrees of openness in a way that gives you the freedom to invent and establishes your ability to make a return.

Open data

As a fluid asset, data encourages you to be more open and collaborative. Rapid progress depends on building on the work of others. So how do you allow access to your data, leverage somebody else's or license it?

Defensively, you have to secure it as an asset and create a culture of confidentiality. Offensively, you will create your own capabilities for modelling and analysis. Then be clear about who can use the results.

As a smaller venture, the main step is to start putting these steps in place for transparent agreements with your partners. It will give you a system of consents that establishes what you can do with the data, who can make what analysis and who can develop products from it. If you can put such a structure in place, then data can live up to the potential that the OECD has identified for it becoming one of the primary inputs to innovation.

Open source

In software, 80 percent of any innovation is open source developed within a community. It's then down to you how creative and profitable the rest of it becomes.

Within open source, there is a spectrum of licences, some highly liberal, others more restrictive. As well as being clear on your legal position, you will take a view at what speed and in what manner the software has been developed.

Open source fundamentally depends on how the copyright is created and shared between everyone in the community. In some instances, you are free to develop whatever you like without attribution. In others, you are required to feedback whatever improvements you make, referred to as copyleft in the Linux community.

Open standards

Open standards are a complementary domain that operate in a different way. It's largely a question of leveraging what is already there, such as WiFi or 5G, then making the case for any future requirements by engaging in industry consortia. The underlying IP is generally based on a pool of patents. Terms of access vary. In some cases, such as Bluetooth, the standard was developed by manufactuers, such as Ericcson, to encourage the sale of hardware. In other, such as cellular networks, a standard royalty (Frand) applies.

Business models

Once you know where you sit on the open spectrum, you gain the flexibility to adopt different business models to give yourself more freedom for creative manoeuvre, while retaining control of your underlying assets. Examples include:

- **Co-creation**: where equal partners from different domains come together to create new value across different disciplines and different cultures.

- **Free standards**: where you release a platform technology to create an ecosystem of second and third movers around you (as Google has done with the Android system for mobiles).

- **Licensing to self-fund**: where you release a platform technology to other domains to fund the development of your core product.

- **Data repositories**: all those in an ecosystem, whether as enterprises or as public bodies, pool their data, aligning its security first, then clarifying its use for analytics and modelling.

- **Supplier interfaces**: where you change the conversation with suppliers to allow for more co-development.

- **MVPs**: where a foundational idea goes through a series of rapid iterations with potential users to identify the minimum viable proposition that the market will accept.

- **Double-sided offers**: where you market a product for free to attract enough followers whose data you can commercialise.

- **Freemiums:** where you release the basic version for free, then charge a premium for upgrading to a premium service.

All of these depend on a different configuration of openness. They are far removed from the traditional push of a technology into the market, where the IP acts as a safeguard. Instead, a more dynamic interaction happens with a broader range of actors, whether users, suppliers or partners, which gives full scope to market pull and gives IP, in all its forms, a primary role in establishing a value proposition that will secure a return for each layer of innovation.

As we saw with Red Hat, which operated through a series of relatively restrictive copyleft licences, it is possible to create a business model that can result in a multi-billion dollar sale to IBM. For all ventures, it's within their power to decide how strategically open they are going to be.

Professor Bowman Heiden is co-director of CIP (the Centre for Intellectual Property), a specialist in knowledge-based business development run jointly by the University of Gothenburg, Chalmers University of Technology and the Norwegian University for Science and Technology. He is also executive director of the Tusher Initiative for the Management of Intellectual Capital at UC Berkeley and a fellow at the Classical Liberal Institute at the NYU School of Law.

Sources

· 'Making Open Innovation Work', a presentation by Bowman Heiden, CIP, Maaike van Velzen, partner, Deloitte and Jimmy Ahlberg, director, open source policy at Ericsson at the High-growth Technology Business Conference, EPO and LESI, November 2022. Full recording at: epo.org/en/news-events

· 'Strategic Openness: Designing open innovation and intellectual property', Bowman Heiden, Bulletin 8, European IP Helpdesk

· 'Catch the Growth Wave of Innovation', an article by Bowman Heiden and Ruud Peters in *Managing High-Growth Intellectual Property*, Novaro Publishing, January 2021

3

REALISING THE VALUE IN DEEP-TECH INNOVATION

As a pioneer of European seed capital for deep tech, Stephan Rauscher at Earlybird-X regularly encounters eight IP hurdles in spinning out ventures from technical universities

Four years into investing €75 million into spin-offs from European deep tech, Stephan Rauscher and his colleagues at Earlybird-X are making a multiple of 2.7. Of their 20 investments, one is worth €100 million, following three funding rounds in quick succession; one has risen in value by ten; another by three; one went bust almost immediately; and one has stalled following the unexpected death of one of the founders. Such highs and lows are an inevitable part of being such an early investor in deep tech.

Although it has taken persistence to reach this point, Rauscher remains convinced of the potential for Europe's deep tech: it produces the same number of graduates as the United States from its top 100 universities, but 30 percent fewer spin-offs and 75 percent fewer unicorns (or ventures that reach a value of €1 billion). For him, there is little point in having a thousand horsepower engine, if you only travel at 50 kilometres per hour.

Unicorns is not a term he particularly likes, however. For him, at these early stages, it's less about identifying data points that translate into future value. Instead, it's more about the system for identifying a stellar technology, matching it to a market of €10 billion or more and finding the right team of founders.

Originally a consultant and a banker in Switzerland, schooled in the management of risk, he first followed up his instinct for the value in European deep tech by observing what was happening around the Technical University of Aachen, before acquainting himself with one of Europe's most successful ecosystems for high-growth spin-offs at the Technical University of Munich.

In 2017, he launched his first version of a seed capital fund which funds spin-offs at the point when they have proved their concept, typically with a grant of €20,000. As a newcomer, it took him time to get going, until he partnered with Earlybird, a venture capitalist that invests in scale-up funding for European tech. Since 2021, his fund, Earlybird-X has been making investments of typically €1 million for a 10 percent stake in spin-offs in areas such as quantum computing, artificial intelligence, mobility and, most successfully, in direct air capture. As a closed end fund, the aim is to finish making investments by 2026 and then spend the next five years realising the value.

Earlybird-X liaises with 25 different European research universities and its team of nine specialise in different areas of technology in consultation with over a hundred professors. For each investment, they recruit a partner from industry as an investor and advisor.

At such an early stage, these ventures are unpredictable, but Rauscher's aim is to be ahead of the conversation as far as possible. So far, he estimates that Earlybird-X has seen over a thousand proposals for spin-offs. Their quality and presentation is highly variable. The challenge is to spot the genuine game changers.

So what has Rauscher learnt from this experience of screening and spinning off deep tech? What are the hurdles to negotiating the IP as an underlying asset? What are the showstoppers that bring deals to a halt? What are the warning signals he has observed? And what advice does he have for founders?

Eight challenges in transferring IP from universities

Speaking at the summit of the EPO and LESI's High-growth Tech Business campaign (November 2022), Rauscher highlighted eight criteria for transferring deep-tech assets into spin-offs with the potential for high growth.

Timing

Spin-offs can only happen if everyone is transparent about their sense of timing: where do you want to go in the next one to five years? and what could limit you? Once you know where you would like to end up and how you might realistically get there, you can make better IP decisions. How, for instance, are you going to balance the competing objectives of commercialising your IP as early as possible and waiting long enough for it to be tangible and robust enough?

Ownership

At the start, ownership of the IP usually rests with the university, although others may have claims. Transfers happen through licence or by assignment to the founders. As no one can know for sure how the tech will perform, the terms of a licence are difficult to set and payments are often relatively high. Alternatively, the cost of buying the IP can drain a spin-off of cash that it might otherwise use for development. A set of European guidelines is in place, although their interpretation can vary from institution to institution: in some research hotspots, it all happens smoothly, although costs can be high; in some more out-of-the-way schools, it can be slower, but less expensive.

University rights

A university may wish to retain some rights in the technology or exercise some restrictions over its use. It may be also be thinking about spinning off other ventures. It always becomes a major point of discussions, which can end up as a no go for the investor.

Protection

The spin-off has to line up its IP so it can withstand any challenge to its ownership. It's worth spending time in the early stages to settle the future, rather than finding yourself compromised in two to three years.

Investor considerations

At the start, it is easy to promise to reward early supporters. Some public agencies might even expect a slice of the IP. However, for founders, it is essential to be aware of the impact of external investment and the dilution of their control. In each funding round, investors will become progressively less tolerant of any messiness or ambiguity. As a seed investor, the challenge for Earlybird-X is not just to identify a technology that can scale, but to find someone who will buy the shares to fund the next stage of a venture's growth.

Valuation

Opinions can vary widely about the IP's value. As it is such an early stage, you can't be too fixed in your assumptions. When so much is unknown, it is hard to rely on the discounted cash flow model and you don't want to deter the founders by setting it too high. Instead, Rauscher and his colleagues take a view of the team, the tech and the market. With the right timing, it gives them a notional value for the venture, from which an estimate of what the IP is worth can be drawn.

Regulatory

Approvals can vary widely from country to country, which is why it is such a significant part of the check that Earlybird-X makes. If, for instance, a technology is deemed part of a critical technical infrastructure, it might mean national partners joining the share register on unfavourable terms.

Follow-on rights

All these questions are not just a question for the university, the founders and the seed investor. If all goes to plan, they will have consequences for future rounds of funding to scale up. A seed investor might tolerate some messiness in the capitalisation table. Follow-on investors will be progressively more stringent: contracts must be crystal clear and the data room spotlessly clean.

Tripwires

Each of these criteria present challenges in themselves. In combination, they can sink a deal, such as when two universities with competing views are involved as co-owners. For Earlybird-X, it was a case of painful delays for the spin-off. Universities may not be speedboats, but decisions that take months will drain a spin-off's cash and stall its momentum.

In this case, one university wanted to license the IP and the other to sell it, which led to an impasse of 18 months. If they had been more transparent at the start, they might have done what was best for the venture as a whole. Ultimately, after the spin-off had laid off people and lost an investor, a way was found to reconcile the two positions.

Each way of commercialising IP has its pros and cons. Acquisition gives the spin-off certainty, but will drain its capital. A licence is hard to negotiate, involves a series of recurring payments and may give the university future rights in the technology.

The alternative is for universities to take equity in the venture. However, you do not want to burden a spin-out with too much of a legacy and, if the university becomes part of the governance, it can

24

affect the agility that you want to encourage. Similarly, professors often expect a stake in the new venture to reflect their role in directing the original research. However, they are likely to playing a progressively less influential role in the future.

A variation is to issue virtual shares in the same way as you might with talent that you want to attract. In the event of a high-yield sale of the shares, a special payment can be made to the university or to the professor. The advantage is that the spin-off has more freedom to make its own decisions and pivot as necessary.

An argument might even be made for the free transfer of the IP, as long as it's not interpreted as state aid. For the university, the advantage is that it will reinforce its reputation as a hub and strengthen its attractions as a destination for further research.

Founders

In Europe, guidelines might be in place for IP transfers, but practice is much more fragmented and deals can break down at numerous points. So what steps can the founders of spin-offs take in Rauscher's experience?

Think about IP from day one

As a founder, you'll face a series of IP challenges, not just in securing the investment, but after it as well. So it's best to start thinking about it from the start. What is your competitive landscape? Is your technology a standalone? Can it be developed further?

Balance your team

Seed investors are less likely to invest in solo founders or in a couple. Too much can go wrong, when so much relies on what the founding team can deliver. The preference is usually for a team of three founders who can between them take the venture forward. Or, in the case of the spin-off that Earlybird-X funded that is now worth €100 million, someone who has the experience of doing it all before.

Reach out early

Founders may feel their product might not be finalised and things may still be missing, but it makes a difference if they reach out early to investors. Together, they have a better chance to check out the market, plug into networks and help find future customers.

Don't become too fuzzy

As a founder, your relations with the university might remain fuzzy for a while. You might still be in the lab or on campus, but you are on the way to becoming a separate operation with a distinctly different set of interests.

Clean up the share register

Right at the start, founders will have support from family, friends and colleagues. Take care in cluttering up the share register too much. The cleaner it is for big investors in later rounds, the better. They will expect your data room to be as clean as possible.

Stefan Rauscher is a partner at Earlybird-X, which backs deep-tech innovation in its early stages, tapping into a network of leading European universities. Investments include spin-offs in quantum computing, artificial intelligence, construction tech, mobility and space.

Sources

· Stefan Rauscher was speaking about turning deep tech into financial assets at the High-growth Technology Business Conference, EPO and LESI, November 2022.
· 'Four Ways to Accelerate Tech Transfer in Europe', Natalia Ahmadian and Frédéric du Bois-Reymond, Earlybird-X, *Medium*, January 2023

4

CROSSING TECH'S
VALLEY OF DEATH

In origin, breakthrough innovations might be shifting decisively from corporate labs to university research, but only an eighth of this intellectual property makes it across tech's valley of death. Ed Cole discusses the prospects for finding more star commercialisers

In deep tech, few innovations make it across the valley of death: the gap between research and the market. Even in the United States, estimates suggest that only 16 percent of the value created in research is released through licensing or equity (*Knowledge at Wharton*, January 2021).

Researchers lack support and don't have the entrepreneurial skills it takes to become commercially involved. Investors are deterred by the high risks of commercialising early-stage research. Universities are guided by policies that expect too much equity, sometimes as high as 50 percent, further deterring investors. The IP that is created remains unused. So what can we learn from ventures that have found their way across tech's valley of death? and is there a way to replicate their performance for future ventures?

Glorious exceptions

At Oxford Brookes University in the 1990s, well before the start of knowledge exchange and technology transfer as widespread standalone disciplines, this cycle was broken by research into antibodies that is now being widely used to test for Downs Syndrome and ovarian reserves, as an indicator of fertility. Through a series of creative commercial steps, including a material transfer agreement, a joint venture, a cross-licence and an acquisition, Oxford Brookes is still earning royalties of £6 million a year. Even if it's a modern university founded in the 1990s, this income puts it financially among the UK's research elite.

It began with an inspirational professor, Nigel Groome, developing an unusually large portfolio of 60 antibodies with the potential for use as treatments or in diagnostics. It was scientifically impressive, but would have no value commercially, unless applications could be found.

So researchers elsewhere were involved through material transfer agreements, which gave them access to the knowledge on condition all modifications were returned to Oxford Brookes. The results were marketed through a distributor, Biorad, which unusually created a joint venture with the university, Oxford Bio Innovation. Both partners seconded it people and it operated from the campus, before becoming a standalone company.

The rights in a selection of its antibodies were then licensed to a company in the US, Diagnostic Systems Laboratories, and a cross-licence was agreed with the Australian owner of a master patent that could have otherwise blocked any future developments. DSL then consolidated everything by buying Oxford Bio Innovation, as well as the Australian patent owner, before selling itself to a pharma major, Beckman Coulter.

To reach this position, Oxford Brookes had already taken two unusual steps for a university: setting up a joint venture and agreeing a cross-licence. Now it completed a third by agreeing a royalty with Beckman Coulter on any sales that used one of four inputs: the patents, the cell lines, the antibodies or the know-how. It's a deal that is still going strong and an example of how to innovate around problems about bringing a technology to market. In this case, a whole suite of intellectual assets, such as patents, copyrights, trade marks, trade secrets, designs, data and competitor analysis, were deployed in making a robust, high-value deal.

Innovation's big shift

In his research at Wharton Business School, Professor David Hsu has identified a strengthening trend for universities to produce pathbreaking innovation across many disciplines. 'We're past the age of corporate R&D labs,' he says. 'All that is business history.'

Instead, modern research universities, he argues, 'tend to be increasingly interested in translating academic research into something that makes a social impact, with associated economic development considerations. That's a big shift.'

'We're talking about not just incremental innovations that could be done elsewhere, but rather more fundamental research at universities,' he says. 'In terms of the quality and quantity of their inventions, they are much more basic, much more original, and have many more forward citations. There are many more claims. This is all true of university patents as compared to corporate patents.'

On average, according to his calculations, universities capture 16 percent of the value they help create through licensing revenues or equity stakes in the start-ups that their research spawns. Within those figures, it appears that some researchers and universities are much better able to commercialise their discoveries than others.

He has isolated two factors that shape this commercial landscape. One is the degree to which an academic team is interdisciplinary. The second is the presence of a star commercialiser.

'Interestingly enough, it's not the star academic that is correlated with commercialisation,' says Hsu. 'It's the star commercialiser, those with substantial prior experience bringing products to market via start-up formation.'

Star commercialisers

It's a pattern that Oxford Brookes has started to recognise. In the 13 years to 2020, it didn't spin out any further innovations. So, instead of relying on one-off inspirations, it joined a pre-acceleration programme, ICURe, that seeks to take promising innovations from British universities across the valley of death by equipping researchers with the entrepreneurial skills to derisk their technologies, plan a start-up and make a convincing case to investors.

In 2018, a PhD spin-off from the University of Bristol, Ziylo, which had been on the ICURe programmes, was sold to Novo Nordisk for £632 million ($800 million). Its synthetic molecules promise to open up the next generation of treatments for diabetes by remaining latent in the bloodstream until triggered by a rise in glucose. For Novo Nordisk, the premium was justified by keeping its lead in treating the 380 million people who suffer from diabetes worldwide.

It's a headline deal, of course, although over the last ten years ICURe has coached 3000 researchers, leading to 320 spin-offs that have so far raised investment of £600 million. So how do they go about helping researchers to test and validate their innovations?

First, they have to apply. Then they will join a boot camp with their cohort to learn about how business thinks and how they can express the value they offer, not just to investors, but to everyone in the industry. They'll be making a lot of assumptions by now, so they are given £35,000 over three months to test their value propositions to explore how the real world responds to their innovations.

During this process, they are mentored in a team of four: an entrepreneurial lead, a business advisor, a principal investigator and a tech transfer professional. After checking their value proposition with the market, they then present to a panel that will give them one of three recommendations: create a spin-off, offer a licence or do some more follow-up work. They might not become as much of a commercial star as Ziylo, whose academic founders are now continuing their research in a new spin-off, but they will be significantly closer to translating their research into use.

IP rights

Depending on the outcome from the panel, postgrad commercialisers may well find themselves in discussions with their universities about the equity in a potential spin-off. At the top level, a vigorous debate has now started about what a share a university should expect.

Historically, the benchmark was 50 percent, based on the classical assumption that the university had taken the lead in derisking the technology. In practice, many investors are deterred by the size of such a stake, so 30 percent might be more usual, as it is only the start of a long commercial process.

A recent report by British university leaders is now even making the case for between 10 and 25 percent for IP-rich ventures and 10 percent for less intensive ones. In some of the major universities in the US, the trend now is toward taking 5 percent in non-dilutable shares.

In a deal as gamechanging as for Oxford Brookes, the process is often more creative and fluid. Even if the patents in its platform technologies have now expired, it is still being paid a royalty for its know-how. It will only lapse when an alternative technology is taken through the whole process of testing and approval. Instead of narrowly defining its IP as a fixed asset, it relied instead on becoming a commercial star, a policy which will continue to benefit the university for many years to come.

ICURe (Innovation to Commercialisation of University Research) is an Innovate UK programme that gives researchers the chance to turn ground-breaking research into investment-ready spin-off companies and licensing deals by providing training and funding. It offers four connected programmes that allow researchers to participate at any stage of their research: (i) Engage at ideation; (ii) Discover for technology readiness level 1 to 4 and commercialisation readiness levels for start-ups 1 to 3; (iii) Explore for research at TRL 2 to 6, CRL 2 to 5; and (iv) Exploit for research at TRL 2 to 6 and CRL 4 to 6.

Dr Edward Cole is ICURe's head of hub in London and south-east England. He was formerly IP and commercialisation manager in the research, innovation and enterprise directorate at Oxford Brookes University, where he has now become a consultant.

Sources

· 'Should universities try to capture more value from their research?', *Knowledge at Wharton*, January 2021
· *Independent review of university spin-out companies*, Professor Irene Treacy and Dr Andrew Williamson, Department for Sciene, Innovation and Technology / HM Treasury, November 2023

5

INNOVATING FOR
BREAK-OUT VALUE

Give your IP the agility to put purpose before solution and open up the potential for multiplying its value, not once but several times, says Robert Klinski at Patentship

For now, you might still be able to afford to innovate in the classical way. Research a technology. Engineer an application. Secure the intellectual property in the solution. However, at each stage, you are going to find value leaking away.

Money is spent on exploring technologies with no certainty of making a return. It is then up to the engineers to find a purpose for it. Typically, 97 percent of the IP that you file will never show a return. The calculation is that it won't matter: the 3 percent more than compensates.

In any case, the IP is such a comparatively minor cost compared to research, development, production and marketing that it can easily be absorbed without anyone taking too much account of it. It represents a comfortable, if wasteful, equilibrium for everyone.

As a model, it is becoming less and less sustainable. Innovation is being turned on its head. The break-out value lies in the early, disruptive stages. It depends on defining the problem first. Where is the pain being felt by the customer? What is the problem you can solve? Once you define your purpose, you can then trigger the scientists or engineers to find a solution. It's a pattern that disruptors have followed for some time and which industrials like Siemens are starting to adopt.

You cannot expect engineers to be radical thinkers. Their role is to implement solutions, not create them. However, the resulting IP then arrives on a market that has already started to grow. Inevitably, you will find yourself competing against other solutions. Yes, you will have your share of the growth, but it will fall well short of the dominance that IP has the capability to deliver.

Over the last 20 years, valiant efforts have been made to fix these shortcomings. We innovate more openly. We collaborate more fully. However, we remain reluctant to share our best ideas when we aren't sure how they will be owned in future, particularly as the tendency with digital is for much of the value to migrate to the top of the chain. Why innovate if the rewards end up elsewhere?

Nor does open innovation solve the problem of launching IP into a market that is already active. Your returns are inevitably going to be less than stellar.

So how you can solve this dilemma? How can you give yourself the chance of being in at the early disruptive stages of a market when the IP in your solution could sweep all before it? What would happen if you turned your innovation practices upside down and gave more weight to the most agile element in the chain of creating new value, your IP?

As a first step, why not release some of the 97 percent of what you spend on IP that never sees a return? Then give your IP team the freedom to scan the horizon. They have the knowledge to talk to engineers and see what future problems require solutions. Once you find a purpose, the IP can be framed around taking away the pain your customers are going to feel and you can start to talk to your engineers about creating a technical solution that is simple enough to become a product.

Such early-stage IP has the potential to become a disruptive technology that can dominate a market for the next few years. The IP is all within your own domain so there is no question of sharing it. It remains speculative, of course. The IP may well fail. However, you are investing far less that you would in a research programme or a collaboration. So you have more scope to move swiftly to the next potential solution.

By making your IP agile, you are giving yourself a highly efficient option on future growth, as some investors in early-start technologies are starting to recognise. Why fund the whole infrastructure of personnel, premises, exploration and testing in a start-up to test an idea when it is just as likely to fail as IP?

By contrast, IP comes at a fraction of the cost, so you can afford many more failures. If it is agile, you will have already established its purpose. If it gains any traction, you can invest in developing a solution with more certainty than giving a start-up two to three years to prove itself.

So let's see how this logic stands up in an area of technology which has consistently seemed just out of reach: quantum computing.

Quantum value today

The closer quantum computing comes to reality, the more urgent becomes the challenge of managing one of its side effects. Because it so radically transforms processing power, none of the algorithms on which online security has depended up until now will be secure.

Most solutions rely on creating smarter chips: however, they are vulnerable because they are software to software. What if you could create the security in the hardware of a device itself, making it much harder to access?

It's a solution that is being pursued by a team of Polish researchers. What are their options for securing their IP? Do they try to take a patent on a platform technology that may well be superseded? Or do they explore what the market is likely to demand and protect those applications instead?

In this way, they are creating a series of options on high growth. They only have to implement them as and when the market takes off. Otherwise they can drop the application and move onto the next without incurring any costs in trying to take it to market. By thinking about the purpose of their IP first, it gives them the agility to catch a market early.

Innovating with purpose

In this scenario, IP acts as the convenor. As a purely mental discipline, it has the capacity to identify and express a problem after talking to engineers, marketing and sales. You're not inventing out of the blue. You're innovating for a purpose.

You are defining high-level functional solutions without necessarily having to implement them as yet. In the case of quantum computing, you might typically combine the evolution of chip design with trends in hacking to extrapolate what breaches could occur.

You're not sitting around waiting for a genius idea. It's more like triage: you bounce ideas back and forth, until you have something tangible that resonates with the market. Because it's an option that doesn't require testing and implementation as yet, it can create significant value almost immediately. In one case, we filed a patent for €5000 and sold it the next week for €3 million. Other patents may go nowhere, of course. However, it is more efficient than waiting for two years for a start-up to test out the idea.

Once you have proof of concept, you can give your IP to your engineers to invent a solution. That way you can stop yourself burning their time and money unnecessarily.

Establishing IP as an asset

When innovating with purpose, IP holds more appeal for investors: it is held in a series of blocks, each of which has the potential to be first to market and exclude others. The costs of implementation are only incurred once the IP has proved itself.

The upshot is that you can develop each application one by one. If the first one doesn't look like working, then you can switch to the next. Alternatively, you can focus on the most promising candidate, then license or spin out the others.

Because each version of the IP stands alone, you could sell different versions of it two, three or four times, either as a licence or as a start-up. In each case, the buyer will be gaining the rights in a clearly defined asset with an established purpose for potential customers.

Where the value of your IP starts to multiply is when you establish the right to prohibit others from the market. It's partly down to your willingness to litigate, although you could negotiate instead or sell your IP to someone who is ready to take action. What matters is your ability to exercise all those options.

Such agility makes IP a commercial product in itself. As an example in its purest form, look at Huawei, the Chinese telecoms manufacturer, whose products are now largely excluded from Western markets. However, it has remained a highly competitive performer by relying on IP as its primary asset. The same will become increasingly true for most high-growth tech ventures.

Conclusion

At full power, R&D is a magnificent battleship, but it struggles to adjust course. You may be developing groundbreaking technologies, but without a purpose, you will be burning money and time. So redeploy your forces. Make IP agile enough to scan the horizon and link up the insights of your engineers and customers. You can then create a series of options to implement not when growth is already happening, but for when it is about to take off. Even as a small player, it's what gives you the potential to disrupt and dominate.

Robert Klinski is a radical pioneer in the field of IP, known for his unconventional approaches to fostering innovation. As the founder of Patentship, he has carved a niche for himself by empowering visionaries seeking to revolutionise disruptive technologies, whether they are Chinese investors searching for better returns than traditional start-ups, Cambridge spin-offs with dreams of becoming unicorns or German engineers re-inventing how they operate. For more see patentship.de.

6

BUILDING AN INNOVATION
SYSTEM FOR SERIAL EXITS

Medtech entrepreneur, Ghassan Kassab, who sold his first invention for over $30 million, is creating an innovation system that has so far produced four licences for medtech majors, six spin-offs and multiple IP options for future deals. Juergen Graner highlights five takeaways for building an innovation system

Most university professors with an endowed chair who invent a new technology and sell it for more than $30 million in their late forties would likely consider early retirement. Not so, Dr Ghassan Kassab. He left academia, using the money to build an innovation system that continues to bring new inventions to market to improve the health of patients globally.

Ghassan was a born fighter. He grew up in Iraq as the son of a nurse with a father that passed away at the age of three, who came with his family to the United States at the age of twelve, having a fresh start in a new country with a new language and new surroundings. He did not go to a prestigious high school, but he understood that if he could advance his knowledge, he might be able to achieve great things. Ghassan excelled in his studies and received his bachelor's degree in chemical engineering, his master's degree in engineering sciences and finished strong with a PhD in bioengineering (summa cum laude), all from UCSD (University of California, San Diego), one of the top schools for bioengineering. Besides training his mind, he also trained his body and earned a fifth-degree black belt in *Shorinji Kempo*.

After his studies Ghassan pursued an academic career that spanned over 20 years, starting from UCSD, then UCI (University of California, Irvine), leading to an endowed chair position at Indiana University/ Purdue University, Indiana. During the latter part of his academic career Ghassan invented a new technology that helps clinicians to find the correct pathway towards the heart with a simple electrical signal. Since he could not find anyone to fund his new invention, he invested himself into the development of the prototype and secured it with a strong patent portfolio. Although he never took it through clinical trials, a company acquired his early-stage technology for over $30 million, providing him with a 30-times return on his investment. Instead of retirement, Ghassan decided to use those funds to change his career from academia to entrepreneur at the age of 48.

During his academic career in Indiana, Ghassan had founded 3DT Holdings in 2006, which was the first cornerstone of his innovation system. Initially the primary function of this company was to act as an IP holding to secure Ghassan's personal inventions. In 2014, Ghassan left his academic career to fully follow his entrepreneurial drive and moved to California. There he established the second cornerstone of his innovation system, CALMI (California Medical Innovations Institute), a non-profit organisation. CALMI provides the research foundation and is focused on the primary interests of Ghassan, which are cardiovascular and gastroenterology applications. As a non-profit organisation, it can tap into a variety of grant options that a for-profit cannot. From the beginning, it has been important to Ghassan to ensure that research at CALMI focuses on medical technologies that have a clear commercialisation pathway to benefit patients globally, something that is not necessarily common in an academic environment.

Today 3DT has evolved and became a fully fledged technology incubator, taking the foundations created at CALMI and developing those into actual products that can be taken all the way through approval at the US regulator, the FDA, and get them ready for market. While 3DT has its own core development team, including engineers, each promising technology is put into a separate legal entity that can tap into all necessary resources. Each technology has its own path to commercialisation without sacrificing the know-how it has acquired through the ecosystem. It works both for Ghassan, as tribal knowledge can be kept and used for additional projects without having to rebuild a team, and for potential acquirers, who do not have to take over a development team that is likely no longer needed, since the products are already FDA approved and ready to market. 3DT is different from other incubators, as it only incubates internal projects, although on occasion it offers its capabilities to friendly partners from the larger network of 3DT.

While advancing technologies in 3DT, Ghassan realised that a third cornerstone was needed to efficiently bring products to a market-ready state. He therefore established Acculab Lifesciences, which is a contract research organisation (CRO) that provides pre-clinical services, including GLP-based studies. It became obvious that existing CROs were cumbersome as partners. Therefore AccuLab was established as a highly efficient and flexible organisation that can provide the needed services faster and at a more competitive price to 3DT's ventures. While initially the intention was to provide services only to 3DT companies, later on it was decided that those pre-clinical services would be offered to third parties at large, whether to early-stage ventures in medical devices and biotech or to larger companies.

The whole innovation system that Ghassan has built, combining engines for research (CALMI) and for development in the form of an incubator (3DT) and a pre-clinical CRO (Acculab), allows him to continuously develop new technologies and get them ready for patients' bedside. Currently 3DT has four exclusive licenses with major medical device corporations and six spin-offs that are advancing technologies with the goal of making serial exists. Profits generated from Acculab's offer to third parties combined with 3DT's licensing income and sale of its spin-offs are put back into the innovation system and, together with the NIH grants obtained from Small Business Innovation Research through 3DT, provide a sustainable model to continuously bring new medical technologies to the market.

From the start, patents have played an integral part in the commercial success of this innovation system. The initial sale of Ghassan's technology for over $30 million before clinical trials would simply not have been possible without them. Also exclusive licensing deals and company exits of the spin-off ventures require a strong IP portfolio. 3DT therefore not only has an internal IP function, it also regularly hires development engineers and scientists to invent around the patents, which in turn results in additional patents for 3DT. Ghassan himself has over 300 issued and pending patents in his name, more than many medium-sized companies.

At a meeting of the High-growth Technology Business Forum in June 2023 with the help of a global expert panel, the following five takeaways were highlighted for those looking to follow the innovative lead that Ghassan has given.

Takeaway 1: great products come from interdisciplinary efforts between scientists, engineers and clinicians

Medtech inventors often fall into the trap of confining themselves to only one area of expertise when they develop their products. If they are scientists they tend to continue to surround themselves with other scientists and keep on working on new types of concepts that may not be relevant for clinical practice. If they are engineers they tend to surround themselves with other engineers and keep on developing new types of products with ever increasing features ending up with products that are perfect, but too expensive and complicated to be practical for clinicians to use given existing cost reimbursement regimes and training options. If they are clinicians, they tend to surround themselves with other clinicians and keep on testing different prototypes that may have great clinical use, but lack a sound engineering foundation that ensures consistent product functionality at a quality level that any market approval may require.

In general people tend to associate themselves with people that are similar and are in the same field. However, great products come from interdisciplinary efforts. Having scientists, engineers and clinicians work hand in hand as they develop their medical devices is key to having products that will have a chance on the market and will have a positive impact on patients and their health. It further makes sense to add regulatory, IP and marketing specialists to such an interdisciplinary team to ensure that your development can be approved by the authorities, properly protected against competitive threats and spark early interest in the market.

Takeaway 2: find the balance between trade secrets, patents and brands to leverage your IP portfolio at each growth point

Know and understand the potential and limitations of your IP portfolio and continuously match it with the requirements of your next stage of growth. Especially in the high-tech field where the development of products is the foundation of the business but financial resources are limited, it makes sense to have fewer and stronger patents, but more trade secrets. However, it is important that even in an early stage of a high-tech venture you need to have at least one cornerstone patent, since investors will require it, besides making sense in the long run to keep copycats at a distance.

As the company grows and has more financial resources, more trade secrets can be converted to patents. The right mix between patents and trade secrets depends on stage of development, market requirements, re-engineering options and intended commercialisation routes. If the intention is to sell the technology at an early stage through a technology divestment, a broader patent portfolio is necessary. The same holds true if a licensing arrangement is sought. In both cases operational excellence matters less, except when the company itself needs it to advance the technology to the point where a deal to divest or license is possible. If the intention on the other hand is to build a technology platform that may be commercialised through several spin-offs with serial exits, then trade secrets and operational excellence play a much more prominent role.

Brands often end up as equally significant, although science and engineering driven companies have the tendency to forget them early on, even if it is basically the same as building a reputation. The market should know and understand what a company represents. This brand not only needs to be built, it also needs to be protected through use and trade mark registrations.

In the early evolution of a business, the brand helps to bring in development partners and investors. As the business grows and products enter the market, a brand that is managed well and built with consistent messaging is key to building market pull for your products in the market. For commercialisation through technology divestment and licensing, the role of the brand is primarily to be able to be taken more seriously by potential buyers or licensees. In most cases they will use their own brand to bring the product to market. If the strategy is to go to market with your own company, then the brand matters more in the long run.

Takeaway 3: create an array of paths to market by combining research and development

Bringing devices to market in the healthcare field can be particularly challenging, no matter if the chosen path is through technology divestment, licensing or spin-off venturing. Innovations can only be provided to physicians or patients after a stringent regulatory process (governed by the FDA in the US). Ghassan has developed a model to bring medical devices to market by building an innovation system that combines a research engine with a development engine that works hand in hand to develop the right products suitable for the market and get them approved by the regulatory authorities. Having all of this in one connected system, allowing product advancement to flow between research and development until the final product is ready for the market, is a great foundation for those that want to develop more than just one product. Allowing third parties to use certain services for a fee and returning financial gains back to the innovation system creates a sustainable model to continuously develop further great products with a variety of applications. While this innovation system developed by Ghassan cannot be protected through patents as such, the operational excellence component that is the glue making this system work in a way unmatched for efficiency provides natural protection against competitors.

Takeaway 4: for high returns from strategic transactions, create IP that can be protected, meets a real need and has commercial value

Many inventors fall in love with their ideas early on. While this love often creates an environment where teams thrive and get intrinsic motivation over and above financial remuneration, it often also provides certain blindness to market needs. There are countless companies that develop great products, where the IP is thoroughly protected, but there is simply no product-market fit. The products may have great features, but most of them may not be relevant or not just understood by the users, be they physicians or patients. This in addition may make products unnecessarily expensive and they cannot be made available to patients, because insurance systems, either private or government driven, are not willing to pay for it. The result is that the product will not be available to the broadest possible pool of patients whose condition the underlying technology could resolve. So, from the early stage of invention through research all the way to development through engineering and regulatory approval, ensure the ultimate use case remains the core driver. Any strategic transaction with high financial returns depends on having a product that serves a real need at a price that customers are able and willing to pay. It is what all buyers of technologies, licensees and acquirers of companies expect.

Takeaway 5: an exit does not always involve the whole business, but divestments, licences and spin-offs too

The general understanding of an exit is that you sell your business and then you either retire or start another one. If the next business route is chosen, then usually it cannot be in the same field for a number of years, since such a limitation is almost always put on sellers of companies by their buyers. However, as with Ghassan, there are other routes to exit.

If you have strong IP then you may be able to simply sell your technology with the patents and know-how to an interested party. The advantage is that you can focus on the technology side and the purchaser will then concentrate on bringing it to market. The disadvantage is that the technology that you have sold could easily be shelved by the buyer to protect their existing revenue stream with an inferior, but more profitable technology. You simply have no control over what the buyer will do with it, although anti-shelving clauses in the contract may help to partially mitigate that risk.

Another pathway to commercialise strong IP is to license it to a third party that will then bring it to certain market. Like a technology divestment, the licensing route monetises technologies that have not yet been brought to market, which may not be within the skill set or the logistics of science or engineering companies. The advantage of a licensing deal versus a technology divestment is that you can build in mechanisms to the agreement that the buyer will have to make a certain effort to bring the product to market. The disadvantage is that you do not have many levers left once you have signed the licensing deal, except those terms that have been negotiated as anti-shelving regulations. Often these mechanisms only give you modest control of how quickly and broadly the product is commercialised.

Especially when you have a platform technology, or, as is the case with Ghassan, you have an innovation system with multiple potential products, then spin-off venturing may be the pathway to choose, which also allows for serial exits. In this case you establish a separate legal entity for each technology or its application. The advantage is that by advancing your technologies through spin-off ventures you have more control over the process until you exit and sell the company, as opposed to technology divestments or licensing arrangements. Moreover, you can find partners and investors for each spin-off separately, individualising structures, depending on how each technology will be brought to market.

When products are not just completed from a development and regulatory approval perspective, but also brought to market at least within a controlled target group that shows market pick-up before an exit, then you have the possibility of moving beyond technology push to market pull that might make you more money, as well as improving the prospects for the buyer of your technology. The disadvantage is that it takes patience, as well as adding marketing and sales to your capabilities in R&D.

For Ghassan, the motivation for creating this innovation system is twofold: 'first, help as many people as we possibly can and then, second, if we reap some rewards, we put them back into the system to give ourselves longevity'.

This article is based on an online live case study event (HTB Forum), which was broadcast on 29 June 2023. The HTB Forum was hosted by the EPO in collaboration with LESI. The event was chaired by **Juergen Graner** with an expert panel of **Audrey Yap** (co-founder and managing director of Yusarn Audrey in Singapore), **Patrick Monroe** (mergers and acquisitions lawyer in San Diego, US) and **Irene Fialka** (chief executive of INiTS and managing director of Health Hub Vienna in Austria). The video of the hour-long event can be viewed in full at www.epo.org/3dt.

Juergen is founder and chief executive of Globalator in the US, UK and Austria with a focus on build-to-sell engagements. He has experience as a chief executive in six countries on three continents and, over the course of his career, has coached over a hundred chief executives in creating value with strategic transactions. Juergen has over 25 years of experience teaching executives in the US, Europe and Asia. He speaks at conferences and teaches on the subject of *Transaction Based Growth Management*^{TM}, a concept he developed on how to make strategic transactions (alliances, licensing, spin-offs, acquisitions and divestments) more successful.

7

LICENSING FOR
HIGHER GROWTH

The European Innovation Council is setting out to help solve the paradox of why Europe's globally competitive creation of knowledge and technology results in relatively few high-growth ventures. Licensing is one of the ways up-and-coming ventures can claim their share of the cake for the technical solutions and IP they create

As the innovation process becomes more open, both in creation and in implementation, licensing is assuming a wider strategic role in realising the potential for high growth. As an agreement that grants the use of intellectual property under set terms, it is giving tech owners the ability to lay the foundations for collaborating more widely, while still making sure they receive their fair share for their contribution.

The risk is that licensing is often considered too narrowly at the beginning and managed too loosely at the end, leaving many ventures with the perception of suboptimal returns. They may have treated licensing merely as a fallback option, only realising its strategic importance when the challenges of bringing a product to market became evident. Others may initially be excited about partnering with a major player without considering a plan B, only to see the deal fall apart later, leaving them in a state of uncertainty.

So how can any deep-tech business go about using licensing effectively to govern how IP is shared and returns are reaped under different scenarios? This was the question that the EIC, a major funder of innovative start-ups, explored with the EPO in their joint event for innovative ventures in October 2024 and in an article published in *les Nouvelles* (The Journal of the Licensing Executives Society International, LESI).

Why license?

When IP assets are what makes the difference for most businesses with their technologies, this question is crucial. Nowadays, technology can go viral, being used everywhere at the same time, which makes intellectual assets increasingly strategic. Licensing is usually considered for two prime reasons: access or revenue. In practice, it may result in four distinct types of relationships.

For access, ventures can form an agreement with a development partner, who may contribute capabilities or resources that are lacking. Alternatively, ventures can establish freedom to operate with a technology competitor, avoiding the risk of IP disputes when their product or service enters the market.

For revenue, innovation can be licensed vertically to someone better placed to take it to market: in other words, licensing instead of production or offering services. Alternatively, ventures may also license horizontally outside their own field either to prove the concept or to generate funds to support further growth.

For those able to master the strategic dimensions of licensing, find the right partners, negotiate a fair deal and manage the relationship effectively, it opens up a series of wins, such as:

- Bringing in the expertise to take technology to market.

- Giving partners access to technology, while excluding others.

- Expanding into new geographical markets and industry sectors, often at the same time.

- Continuously improving the value of innovation by contributions from partners.

- Retaining long-term influence on the advancement of technology.

- Lining up minimum and milestone payments regardless of the ultimate commercial success of the licensed technology.

- Covering some or all of the costs of intellectual property protection.

- Keeping a second chance for innovation in reserve in case the primary business model does not achieve the desired goals.

- Sharing in the returns if an innovation becomes part of a commercial breakthrough.

License what?

Strategically, licensing can provide for a portfolio of opportunities. As a first step, it is important to take an expansive view of what IP is involved. A venture might be developing technology to create products or services, devices or materials. It will then design its features and programme how it performs. It will build a brand with logos, web pages and graphics. It will also create the supporting documentation for users. Around all this, a wealth of knowledge about how everything works and can be used most efficiently in practice will be built up.

Patents and trade secrets are usually the foundation for technology, although copyright often also matters for digital assets. Designs, trade marks and know-how can all add significantly to the value of a licence. Although each of these intellectual assets might have a value in itself and be licensed individually, it is the strategic combination of them that makes the licence truly valuable.

Infinite Roots: accelerating take-up

Licensing was not yet in the original business model at Infinite Roots in Hamburg, when it was founded in 2018. The company is building a new generation of natural and sustainable food with mushroom roots and so far has raised over €70 million and employs over 60 people.

Licensing represented a switch in how the company had been thinking about its business strategy. The main attractions were to generate revenues prior to getting regulatory approval for selling their products in Germany, to enter other geographical markets and to expand the company's knowledge of how to scale up the technologies for production. The risk was that they might jeopardise their future growth if any IP escaped.

Help came from two sources. An EIC coach helped them develop this additional business case and a former IP manager from a major chemicals company joined the company as IP lead. Their input was essential for drafting a set of terms in three to four weeks, saving a great deal of time and keeping the momentum going in negotiations.

Two candidates were in the frame as partners: one to extract nutrients from leftovers that are used as a fermentation medium and the other to optimise the fermentation of the mushroom roots. In both cases, it was a matter of dealing with an industry giant who pushed back hard on the terms. However, Infinite Roots' negotiators and leadership team now had a clear grasp of the essentials of payments, the extent of use and what IP was involved, as well as duration, limitations and termination. They were able to define beforehand when to continue negotiations and when to step away, which gave them greater confidence and strengthened their position.

Licensing risks

Licensing can speed up adoption of a technology, take it into new markets and give a venture financial independence. However, it also brings a distinct set of new risks. These can include:

- Potentially enabling a future competitor.

- A value loss if not all relevant intellectual assets are considered. A lack of returns if the deal is not structured carefully with different types of payments.

- A loss of momentum if the venture relies only on one licensee and does not consider anti-shelving provisions.

- Delays as agreeing a licence might take a surprising amount of time and commitment. Typical barriers are a lack of licensing experience and lengthy decision-making processes in larger organisations.

- A disconnect between the licensee's innovation and business teams, which might lead to a licence not being signed or followed up on after all.

- The IP at stake might become vulnerable if the licensing partner selected is not able or prepared, or is reluctant, to defend it.

Linari and the Santa Claus moment

Today, Linari Engineering is a pioneer in nano materials for wind turbines, employing around 25 people and taking the lead on an EIC Transition project. When it was starting out several years ago, it developed a robotic gas knob to remotely control home appliances.

The company got into negotiations with one of the world's largest manufacturers of food appliances, selling several million units a year. They promised to prototype Linari's technology, take it into production and pay Linari a percentage on each sale. It felt like a Santa Claus moment.

Linari spent the next few years working on the prototype with the manufacturer's Italian facility. At that point the project was cancelled, which came as a shock to everyone as it had seemed a highly productive co-operation. The manufacturer's marketing director, who had not been involved, concluded that customers were not ready for it.

As chief executive, Stefano Linari checked his exclusive licence and realised that while it promised attractive financial returns on the upside, it had little to say about non-performance. The manufacturer continued to make modest annual payments until the agreement expired. By then, it was too late for Linari to revive any interest. Too much time and energy had been lost.

Looking back, Stefano Linari acknowledges that he paid too much attention to the patent and developing the technology, and too little to the licensing agreement, which is what ultimately influences the fate of the technology. This experience was a valuable lesson learnt for him and his business, which helped them to successfully navigate future deals. It might seem like Christmas has come, he says, but you should never be afraid to step away from negotiations early, if safeguards against non-performance are not on the table.

Doing the deal

Before you start, it is important to be clear about the ultimate goal and the synergies that could be created: what is the size of the cake you could bake together? Negotiations can then be approached in that light. What outcome matters most? What is the best that could happen? What are the alternatives? What is the fallback? What is the bottom line? What should be avoided at all costs?

Then three further points should be clarified. Firstly, a non-disclosure agreement must be put in place. Secondly, every decision maker on the licensee's side must be aligned, not just the negotiating team, possibly also the board and investors. Finally, there must be clarity on the schedule.

Now the terms the business is looking to reach should be reviewed, resolving points such as:

- What is the business objective being pursued? What activities does the deal cover, what is the object of the licence and what are the fields of use? Generally, one should understand the goals of the other party and aim to give access to what is needed to enable a win-win collaboration, but not to more than what is necessary.

- What is the balance between control and diffusion? How much exclusivity is justified to invest in the joint endeavour? What territories or markets are realistically covered now and will be in the foreseeable future? Can the technology be adopted by an industry more generally in a non-exclusive way?

- What happens if the intended commercialisation does not work out? Can the agreement be terminated? What compensation might be due? Are the rights for improvements secured to keep freedom to operate? And can the technology be transferred to any third party after termination of the license?

- What other services or support to the licensee might be required, like know-how transfer, improvements to the technology, promotion at conferences etc?

- How are improvements to the technology shared, who owns them, who can use them and under what conditions?

- What is the balance between risk and reward that everyone is expecting?

- How will payments be structured as initial costs are incurred, breakeven is reached and profits come into view? Essentially, one should consider a combination of payments made upfront, against milestones, and for minimum and running royalties.

Deals are often more arduous to negotiate than technology creators expect, particularly if they are partnering with one of the leading players in the industry. Schedules can drift, assumptions can change and opportunities can be challenged.

OncoQR: pursuing multiple pathways

OncoQR is a venture based in Austria that has been engaged for several years in solving one of the most pressing challenges in the innovative use of vaccines to treat cancers and allergies: how can antibodies attack unhealthy cells without provoking an immune system over-reaction? Its solution is a so-called 'warhead' that carries the immunogen to a target cell.

The warhead is present in each vaccine, while the treatment for each condition varies and is determined by the composition of the immunogen it carries. OncoQR has the foundational knowledge for these transformative breakthroughs in immunology but lacks the resources to develop each product.

Its strategy is to horizontally license its three main patent families in multiple pathways. In parallel to these licences with its partners, it is developing its own treatment for breast cancer, for which it has its own product patent. So far, the costs of its research have largely been funded from what it has earned from its licences, leveraged by national grants it has been awarded.

Each of these licences covers a specific use case, which allows each partner to operate exclusively within a narrowly defined field. Within its agreements, OncoQR also includes its secret know-how about the warhead and how it is manufactured, as both sides share the same interest in treatments becoming available. If any improvements are then made, a back-licence governs how these are shared freely with OncoQR and other licensees of the warhead, which allows it to continuously increase the value of its technology and ensures freedom to operate. The costs of the product patents are the responsibility of each licensing partner.

Finally, payments to OncoQR take into account the risks of developing treatments; some are made upfront, some against milestones and some as royalties. So far, OncoQR has maintained its financial independence, giving it control over what options to pursue for the technology next.

After the deal

The deal is only ever the start. Licensing is a marathon that can last 20 to 30 years. The people implementing it may well be different from those who negotiated it, so it is worth making sure that everyone is up to speed with the strategy and that the deal is implemented as planned or adjusted to unforeseen developments.

Licensing is only ever the best prediction one can make of the future. In practice, incentives may turn out to be less attractive for one partner if economic realities change in an unexpected way. Sometimes it may be worth remaining open to renegotiating terms to prevent a partnership from failing.

Equally, it makes sense to remain alive to what further value can be created and what happens when it comes to the second or third versions of a product. Everyone in the boat has to keep pulling together. Licensing is a dynamic process that might conclude with one company buying all the assets of another.

The authors of this article were **Thomas Bereuter**, Innovation Networks Manager, European Patent Academy, EPO; **Adéla Dvořáková**, Project Adviser, EIC Transition, EISMEA; and **Viorel Peca**, Head of Unit, EIC Transition, EISMEA.

The EIC-EPO event on licensing-based business models was held on 9 October 2024 with support from the European IP Helpdesk. Speakers included **Viorel Peca**, Head of Unit, EIC Transition; **Patrice Pellegrino**, Director, EPO Brussels Office; **Christian Soltmann**, Product Manager, Patent Data and Services, EPO; **Bowman Heiden**, Director, Centre for Intellectual Property (CIP); **Adéla Dvořáková**, Project Adviser, EIC Transition; **Thomas Bereuter**, Innovation Networks Manager, European Patent Academy, EPO; **Karin Hofmann**, President, Licensing Executives Society Austria, TU Wien; **Sonja London**, President, Licensing Executives Society International, TactoTek; **Natalia Drost**, Strategic Projects Lead, Infinite Roots, and **Stefano Linari**, Chief Executive, Linari Engineering. Find the recordings on the EPO's

YouTube channel (youtube.com/watch?v=a7k16Y_ePek) or on the EIC website (eic.ec.europa.eu/events/licensing-based-business-models-webinar-2024-10-09_en).

The EIC is facilitating more licensing support to innovators in three main formats: access to IP and strategy training; access to licensing experts or mentors; and access to sector specific experts.

An article, 'Empowering the Licensing Capabilities of EIC-funded Start-up Companies' by **John Cosmopoulos, Thomas Bereuter, Anne-Marie Sassen, Francesco Matteucci, Ivan Stefanic, Isabel Obieta** and **Iordanis Arzimanoglou** was published in *les Nouvelles*, the journal of the LESI, in June 2024, available at: epo. org/licensing-business-models.

• *The views expressed in this article are the responsibility of the authors and do not necessarily reflect the views of the European Patent Office, European Commission nor of the European Innovation Council and SMEs Executive Agency. These organisations are not liable for any consequence stemming from the reuse of this article.*

8

AI, ITS ECOSYSTEM AND IP

Samuel Deschamps of Santarelli reviews the surge of AI start-ups and scale-ups that is happening in France, highlighting the cultures for IP and open source that are being adopted within this ecosystem

In the past few years, artificial intelligence has hit the news, as companies such as Alphabet (the parent company of Google), Microsoft, Meta or Nvidia invest heavily in it. In August 2023, Goldman Sachs estimated that AI investment could be approaching $200 billion globally in 2025, most of which is now private.

Smaller firms, such as Mistral AI, Hugging Face and Nabla, have also taken a good position with respect to innovation in AI. In terms of IP, it appears that they do not specifically rely on patenting innovations, mostly developing proprietary algorithms and managing proprietary data instead.

Mistral AI

French newcomer Mistral AI, founded in April 2023 by veterans of Meta Platforms and Google DeepMind, is making waves by championing open-source technology, developing freely available large language models as an alternative to closed-off systems. They secured €385 million in funding by October 2023 and their valuation skyrocketed to over $2 billion by December 2023. In June 2024, they secured an additional €600 million, propelling their valuation to a staggering €5.8 billion. This latest funding round was led by venture capital giant General Catalyst with the participation of existing investors.

Hugging Face

Hugging Face, a French-American company with roots in New York, creates tools for building applications with machine learning (ML). Its claim to fame is the Transformers library, ideal for natural language processing, and a platform for sharing ML models and datasets. Originally founded in Paris in 2016, the company started with a chatbot app for teenagers, but quickly pivoted to become an ML platform. Its dedication to open-source technology is evident in its contributions to large language models like BLOOM, a multilingual powerhouse with 176 billion parameters.

Hugging Face's growth has been impressive. It has secured significant funding rounds, reaching a $4.5 billion valuation by August 2023. Partnerships with tech giants like Amazon Web Services (AWS) and collaborations with Meta to accelerate European AI development showcase their commitment to making AI accessible and fostering innovation.

Nabla

Paris-based start-up Nabla is an ambient AI assistant, designed to take the burden off healthcare professionals and improve patient care. Nabla listens in on your consultations and uses its cutting-edge AI to automatically generate clear, detailed clinical notes that seamlessly integrate with your electronic health record. Developed by top AI researchers alongside practising clinicians, Nabla works across specialties and settings, offering numerous options for customisation to fit any workflow. It is already trusted by over 30,000 clinicians and used by over 40 organisations, making it the most widely implemented ambient AI in healthcare. Its record for constant innovation with the aim of becoming the most intuitive and reliable AI partner for all clinical needs has secured this French start-up $24.1 million in series B funding.

France: a thriving hub for AI in Europe

Inspired by ventures like Mistral AI, Hugging Face and Nabla, France is rapidly becoming a powerhouse for AI in Europe. On 21 May 2024, the French government signalled it as a strategic priority by announcing a €400 million investment fund, Here's a look at how its AI ecosystem is now evolving.

- **Start-up boom**: with over 600 AI start-ups (a 24 percent increase from 2021 to 2023), France boasts a vibrant entrepreneurial scene. Notably, half of these start-ups are already profitable or on track to be within the next three years.

- **Generative AI leadership**: France takes the lead in generative AI with 76 start-ups specialising in creating realistic sounds, text, videos and images.

- **Investment magnet**: AI companies in France secured €3.2 billion in funding in 2022, making it a top destination for investors.

- **Global AI talent**: France is the top choice in Europe for foreign investment projects in AI, highlighting its attractions for AI talent.

- **Home to AI giants**: major players like Google, Meta, Hugging Face, Dataiku, Tata and Accenture have chosen France as their AI research and decision centre.

- **Cutting-edge research**: France is at the forefront of AI research, having developed some of the world's most powerful models, including Llama 2, Llama 3 and Mistral Large.

France's commitment to AI extends beyond current achievements. The Institut Polytechnique de Paris, a prestigious research institution, recently received €70 million to create a world-class AI cluster. This initiative aims to:

- Foster groundbreaking research and innovation in AI.

- Train the next generation of AI experts.

- Develop practical AI applications for societal benefit.

This investment aligns with the France 2030 plan that aims to establish a network of ten internationally recognized AI clusters which will solidify France's position as a global leader in AI research, development and talent.

Based on these solid foundations, we expect to see new AI ventures in France in healthcare, industrial automation and creative industries, such as video games.

AI and IP

AI patents are growing rapidly. According to EPO data, the number of international patent families for core AI rose from 41 in 2008 to 1109 in 2018. However, patenting AI and ML inventions can be challenging, especially in Europe.

AI, as a subset of computer science, falls under the category of computer-implemented inventions (CIIs). These inventions, involving computers or programmable devices, are subject to specific patentability criteria. While software itself is generally excluded from patent protection, inventions incorporating software, including AI, can be patented if they demonstrate a technical character.

The EPO has developed clear guidelines for assessing the patentability of CIIs, including those involving AI. To be patentable, an AI invention must not only meet the criteria of novelty and inventive step, but also provide a technical solution to a technical problem. This technical contribution can be achieved through the application of AI to solve a specific problem in a technical field or through a technically advanced implementation of AI algorithms.

The EPO's examining divisions and its boards of appeal use the two-hurdle and COMVIK approaches to assess the patentability of AI inventions, as confirmed in Decision G1/19 (Pedestrian simulation) by the Enlarged Board of Appeal. Recent versions of the EPO's guidelines for examination also include these criteria.

This framework allows for patent protection in sectors utilising AI, such as medical devices, automotive and aerospace, putting such ventures at an advantage when attracting funding. However, in AI, it appears that traditional IP, such as patents and trade marks, is being combined with the development of proprietary algorithms and with the management of a large amount of proprietary data.

Established industrial firms or luxury brands that wish to enhance their operations by adopting AI face similar challenges with their IP. To remain competitive, they will rely on finding the right combination to manage their algorithms, data and patented innovations.

AI will transform the professional practice of IP as well. For law firms, new AI software such as Harvey, is currently being deployed at scale in large law firms in New York, London and Paris. This kind of software acts as an assistant for lawyers, notably for legal search or the preparation of a first draft on a legal matter. Lawyers in Paris have found that these tools are reducing the time spent revising commercial contracts, for instance, allowing them to improve their level of service.

Also, for patent practices, AI services such as ipQuants, Dolcera, Solve Intelligence or Qatent (acquired by Questel) are proposing new tools to perform tasks, such as drafting patent applications or responding to developments in a case. In the next three to five years, the daily work of IP professionals is likely to be transformed. IP managers in high-growth ventures will also gain from these improvements in productivity and efficiency.

Samuel Deschamps has been active for many years at the intersection of technology and IP, advising innovative SMEs, patent pools, large corporates, research institutions and start-ups. He is a partner of one of the largest and more modern IP practices in France, Santarelli Group. He can be contacted at: s.deschamps@ipside.com and +33 5 33 10 00 20.

9

AI, DRUG DISCOVERY
AND THE POTENTIAL FOR IP

AI routines are powering the discovery of new treatments, even for conditions as severe as Stephen Hawking's. Christoph Behrens and Lukas Bischoff at Meissner Bolte review the potential of AI for creating IP, highlighting how ventures like Insilico are taking a lead

Today, the average person may still wonder how artificial intelligence may impact intellectual property, as the most publicly visible applications, such as ChatGTP, are mainly concerned with the processing of text. Such subject matter is not patentable, as it does not go beyond data processing and visualisation.

However, we are now seeing the emergence of ventures who are capturing the potential for developing and using AI in the generation of IP. One of the forerunners, Insilico Medicine, is using AI to speed up processes (or routines), which were conventionally driven by manual research and serendipity or, in practice, discoveries by unplanned strokes of fortune.

By using such AI routines, Insilico with its academic partners was able to start tackling the disease from which Stephen Hawking most visibly suffered, ALS (amyotrophic lateral sclerosis), which has always been hard to treat. Such identification of potential drugs with AI has so far led to the discovery of 28 new targets in a relatively limited time. One of them, FB1006, is now in clinical trials. Since patents, as an IP asset, are granted on a first-to-file basis, a reduction of the time to identify new drugs and targets is expected to give a significant advantage to companies who follow Insilico in its use of AI.

Where AI and IP have favourable overlap

What enabled Insilico to develop as such a strong player in drug development, when the company was founded only in 2014, and the field is notoriously governed by big pharma companies such as Pfizer, Merck or Novartis? As its initial starting point was in finding an alternative to animal testing for research and development of pharmaceuticals, its later development could probably not have been foreseen. However, since it was interested in the development of AI more generally, it worked its way into drug discovery itself, where the routines, which they had initially developed, can be applied.

Even so, going into AI for generating IP may seem counterintuitive at first sight. The set of rules or algorithms on which AI depends are excluded from most patent laws (including the European).

However, if AI can take over routine tasks such as information processing, which have conventionally been performed by humans, it can benefit the generation of IP. Al is especially suited to the analysis of vast sets of data, where humans falter in seeking the needle in the haystack. Insilico is a good example of how to establish a strong IP position by using AI as a tool to obtain knowledge on which a patent application can be later based.

By pairing AI with IP generation, each development stage is accelerated. Less time is taken to eliminate targets and more attention is given to the most promising candidates. The advantages of Al become apparent in assisting and accelerating the generation of IP, whose subject, a newly developed drug, can then benefit from longer protection to pay off initial investments.

How AI supports drug development

When thinking about implementing Al, a first step is to recall how conventional drug development usually proceeds. Here a protein and the function it performs in the human body are often the starting point for the scientist. Disease in many cases is an imbalance in the interplay of processes in the body. Treatment strategies are mostly targeted at re-establishing this balance, for example, by regulating the function of proteins which are overactive, in which case compounds to deactivate or block the protein are developed.

Such mechanisms rely on competitor molecules that have similarity to a natural substrate of the protein, but which bind more strongly and prevent the protein from performing its current function.

Alternatively, the binding of compounds may initiate a small change in the three-dimensional structure of the protein, which decreases its ability to bind to a natural substrate.

For both mechanisms, the 3D structure makes it possible to perform computer-based docking experiments. Compounds are artificially bound to the protein and the strength between the two is assessed. In this manner, it is possible to screen large compound libraries for their possible binding capabilities.

The bottleneck in this process is finding the 3D protein structures. Conventionally, proteins are crystallised and analysed by x-ray diffraction. However, not all can be crystallised and alternatives are highly expensive. So 3D structures can be hard to establish. Until recently, x-ray structural data had only been available for a small fraction of proteins that represent possible targets for drug development.

AI for protein structure modelling

A pioneer AI routine now predicts the most likely structure of a protein from its amino acid sequence. Alphafold was introduced by DeepMind, a subsidiary of Alphabet, in 2018 and an improved version published in 2020. This programme has become the benchmark for the prediction of all 3D structures in the human genome and is now included in public databases, such as UniProt. For any protein, Alphafold compares its sequence with those that are already known and confirmed. Based on the probable interactions of amino acid residues, it makes a prediction of the most likely structure of the protein.

AI for identifying disease markers

An area at the interface of AI and drug development, where Insilico is active, is the identification of proteins and markers associated with diseases, for which pharmaceuticals or antibodies can be subsequently developed. To this end, Insilico has developed an AI system called PandaOmics, which can analyse data from biological samples on the entirety of genes, proteins or messenger RNA (also called omics data). Comparisons are made between respective datasets from patients, who suffer from a given disease, and healthy people. If expression levels of protein are only found in the patients, they can represent a possible target for the treatment of the disease.

Given the size of datasets that are generated for even a single biological sample, AI has a particularly high potential for this kind of analysis. PandaOmics has been integrated by Insilico into a tool called Pharma.ai. It goes beyond data comparison, searching scientific publications and patents for information relating to a protein of interest, helping to rule out false links between the identified proteins and the disease.

Such AI analysis also has potential to identify patient groups, which may respond to a given treatment, and distinguish them from other patients, who suffer from the same disease, but are not receptive to the treatment. Breast cancer is a notable example. With such information, patients can be prescribed the right medication, which can prevent unwanted progression of the disease due to ineffective treatment.

AI in compound optimisation

A further area, where AI has been used by Insilico, is optimisation of compounds, which have been identified as targets. Here, Insilico has developed a tool called Chemistry42, which can learn from the simulation of the binding of large numbers of compounds to a given protein. Variants of the best binding compounds are generated and tested. In this way, compounds with the highest potential are identified as candidates for clinical phase testing.

Over time, it is expected that such routines will improve, as data from real-life testing is fed back to eliminate inaccurate predictions. The benefits of machine learning apply in particular to the treatment of diseases where there is more insecurity about the true structure and interaction of a given protein with a potential drug.

The Chemistry42 tool is also limited to the prediction of the chemical structure, but it can also can suggest synthetic routes for the production of compounds. It can even be linked to automated devices that can then synthesise the AI-generated compounds.

AI for clinical trial simulation

Insilico is also applying AI to the predictive modelling of clinical trials. Its tool, InClinico, has been trained with information and data from drugs, which have successfully passed clinical trials, as well as those that failed. Its routines are specifically directed at identifying the causes of failure (for example, the molecular substructures of candidates that might give rise to toxicity issues or adverse interactions with other proteins). Early results for predicting the outcomes of clinical trials had a high rate of accuracy, close to 80 percent. As clinical trials are usually the most expensive part of bringing a new drug to a patient, AI routines represent a valuable tool to prioritise the trials of the most promising compounds.

Potential time gains: what is possible with AI

Recently, Insilico has shown what may be possible with AI in drug development. By using a combination of its PandaOmics and Chemistry42 tools, they were able to identify CDK20, as kinase, which is overexpressed in many tumour cell lines including colorectal cancer, lung cancer and ovarian cancer, as a potential target for the treatment of hepatocellular carcinoma (HCC, a form of liver cancer). By using the 3D structure of CDK20 as generated by AlphaFold and Chemistry42 for the generation of possible inhibitor compounds for CDK20, they were able to identify a hit compound with a binding constant of about 9 micrometres. This target was selected with the synthesis and testing of only a single digit number of actual compounds, highlighting what is possible with using respective AI routines. It is no surprise that big pharmaceutical companies are significantly increasing their AI abilities to avoid being left behind.

AI in drug discovery: future developments

For the future, with the respective routines that are now available, a trend towards an integration of all of these routines into one system can be expected, covering all steps of drug discovery, starting from the identification of protein targets for a given disease to the preparation and optimisation of candidates, and then the choice of the most promising compounds for clinical testing.

Does this mean that eventually Al will do all the work in drug discovery? Most probably, it will not be the case as most AI routines have been developed and are trained on the basis of existing knowledge and data, which might be biased so that there is a tendency of Al to provide new data with similar characteristics. However, it can be expected that with time the Al routines will become better and better, so it is likely there will be no way around using such routines in the future.

It is already clear that the use of AI can speed of discovery of new drugs, which brings a huge advantage in term of IP protection. In addition, if by using AI, companies are able to focus on compounds that are on average more likely to reach the market, they will spend less on drug that eventually fail in clinical trials, leaving more financial resources for further research.

AI is speeding up how knowledge is gained as a basis for IP. In pharmaceuticals, what matters is being faster than a competitor. To stay in the game, it's time to drop any reservations about whether artificial simulations are of less benefit to the real life. Access to AI is not limited to those who develop routines like Insilico or big pharma, who have sufficient funds to create their own AI. Routines are available publicly or through licensing. Whereas Al will not solve all problems in drug development, it definitely has the potential to take ahead those who use it far ahead of those who do not.

Meissner Bolte is a full-service IP law firm comprising European, German and UK qualified patent attorneys, as well as brand and litigation specialist lawyers. **Christoph Behrens** has worked in projects involving patent filings, prosecution and litigation in the technology areas of pharmaceuticals, life sciences and chemicals for about 15 years, and has gained extensive experience in both patent prosecution and litigation in these areas. **Lukas Bischoff** is a partner who has worked in chemicals, pharmaceuticals and life sciences for more than nine years. For more details, t + 49-89-212186-0 e: mail@mb.de or www.mb.de.

10

IP-BACKED FINANCING

IP rich with the potential for high growth? Matthew Rodgers at Stratagem reports on how the financing gap for scale-ups is starting to close and how IP is establishing itself as an asset for early-stage ventures to raise money without diluting control

IP-backed financing is a mechanism by which companies seek to raise money against intangible assets, notably intellectual property rather than the more traditional tangible assets, such as land, buildings and machinery. This article aims to provide a brief understanding of what IP-backed financing is, why it is needed and the mechanisms by which it can implemented.

For a number of years the existence of a financing gap has been recognised between traditional companies that are rich in tangible assets, for whom traditional debt financing is routinely available, and more modern, often smaller and faster moving companies, which may not have many tangible assets, but whose business model is backed by intangible assets such as IP.[1] A subset of these companies, high-growth SMEs, in fact represent less than 1 percent of companies in the United Kingdom by volume, but add £1.2 trillion to the economy.[2] Such companies have huge potential to deliver further growth to the economy but have fewer avenues by which to raise money. As the economy moves away from traditional industries towards ones based more on services and technology, this finance gap represents an important impediment to growth, both for the companies themselves and to the economy as a whole. The challenge then, is how do companies raise growth funding, when they have few traditional assets against which banks are typically prepared to lend money?

In the absence of hard assets, the traditional funding route for early-stage companies is equity-based finance from crowdfunding, business angels, venture funds and private equity. At this stage of growth, these companies choose to trade a proportion of the business for the funding necessary to move the business forward. In 2022, a ScaleUp Institute survey[3] indicated that, of high-growth companies that did use equity finance, around 58 percent used venture capital, 58 percent used financing from business angels and 9 percent used crowdfunding.

Whilst IP is a factor in decision-making for equity finance, it is not the most important consideration; equity investors tend to invest in companies and the teams that manage them, not specifically in IP assets, although of course the presence of certain types of IP may be indicative of a strong market position and an analysis of a company's IP position will be a key part of the decision to fund. In some areas, such as technology-focused companies, a strong IP position is a requirement, but this may simply be the ownership of a single key patent application.

Equity finance, of course, dilutes the ownership and control of founders and early investors, so in later rounds of fund raising, companies may not wish to use this approach. Debt-based financing may be the preferred route at this point, because, at least, it keeps the growing company in the hands of founders and early investors. The same ScaleUp Institute survey indicated that some 36 percent of companies chose not to take this route because of issues related to dilution.

Whilst debt finance may be considered the most appropriate route to finance the scale-up phase of some growing companies, banks have traditionally shied away from loaning money against intangible assets such as IP, although it is recognised as an asset, and may be recognised to greater or lesser extent in the decision-making process. At the lower end, IP may simply be one of a number of recognised assets over which a bank may take a security as part of a debt financing deal. At a higher level, a lender may give active consideration to the IP and its value as part of the process, but does not link the loan value to any realisable value of the IP. IP-backed financing falls into a third class, where the IP is given a more formal value and financing is structured around the use of the IP as collateral.

The difficulty that banks face in structuring loans around IP itself is due to a number of factors, including regulatory requirements that govern the criteria for use of assets as collateral, but also because of the difficulty of understanding the value and risks associated with a particular portfolio. With some notable exceptions, IP portfolios are difficult to understand and complex to value, the risks associated with them are perceived to be high, and the ability to realise the asset in the event of default is unclear.

The nature of IP means that its value, in large part, hinges on the value of the market for which it provides exclusivity, the breadth of that exclusivity and the availability of alternative products in that market. Thus a portfolio of patents that effectively excludes competitors from entering a high-value market (and therefore protects a high-value revenue stream) is of greater value than a similar portfolio for a device with several alternatives in a crowded market.

The value of an IP right or indeed a portfolio of rights can change significantly over time for a number of reasons, not least, because some rights, such as patents, copyrights and design rights, have a limited life span and remaining life will have a significant bearing on value. Moreover, those rights that arise from an examination process (eg, patents, designs, trade marks) may fail the examination process or be significantly reduced in scope. It may then not serve to exclude competitors, or worse, it may no longer actually cover the product itself. Once granted, the validity of rights may be challenged by competitors looking to clear the way for their own products and, when asserted in litigation, the rights may be invalidated. On the other hand, the value of a single patent application filed for a pharmaceutical product can increase many fold as the drug passes various development gates towards approval. Robust methods of IP valuation are therefore key to establishing a functional IP-based lending ecosystem.

Parameters for the valuation of tangible assets are well established and, since these types of assets are regularly traded, surveyors have access to models and a large quantity of comparative data. In contrast, the valuation of intangible assets relies on a variety of developing methodologies, often with several distinct methods being used and compared to provide a final value. The analysis relies on detailed accounting approaches but three approaches can be generalised. These are:

- **A market-based approach**: appropriate for specific asset types that are traded or licensed and whose value can be approximated by comparison with recent deals. This approach has been applied to broadcast rights, for example.

- **An income-based model**: this is the most commonly used approach, but, in reality, is a mixture of approaches that takes into account the income, cash flow and/or savings attributable to the IP asset in a variety of ways. These include: an excess-earnings approach that values the asset on the basis of the value of cash flow attributable to the asset after excluding the proportion attributable to other assets; a relief from royalty method that values the asset on the basis of the royalty that would be payable if the asset were licensed from a third party; and a with-and-without method in which the value of a business is calculated where the asset concerned is deployed against the situation where it is not, the difference being the value of the asset.

- **A cost model**: this assesses the cost of replacing the asset. It is obviously a poor model of the value of some types of asset, whose value is many multiples of the cost of replacement or where the asset is a one-off and irreplaceable, but has been used for in-house developed software, where the cost of development is fairly well definable, for example.

In recent years, international standards for the valuation of intangible assets have been developed under the International Valuation Standards Council (IVSC) and are regularly reviewed and updated. The standard relating to intangible assets is International Valuation Standard (IVS)-210.[4]

There is an increasing recognition on the part of governments, including the UK government, of the need for an alternative model for financing the growth of potentially high-growth but tangible-asset-poor companies. This recognition, allied with the understanding that a key subset of these companies have IP assets of a high recognisable value, has encouraged financial institutions to develop mechanisms by which this IP can be used to raise debt finance and to bring IP-backed financing into the mainstream. WIPO has taken an interest in this challenge and has published several discussion documents[5] and encouraged member states to report on their experience as part of a series, *Unlocking IP-backed Financing*. The UK's own report in the area was recently released.[6]

There is now a growing number of financial institutions worldwide offering IP collateralised debt financing options and a number of approaches have emerged, adapted to the type of IP and the borrowers' characteristics. Some examples are provided below.

Pullman bonds: copyright in music

This is a pioneering mechanism developed to leverage royalties in music back catalogues. The approach was developed by David Pullman and David Bowie in 1997 to leverage the rights in 25 of Bowie's early albums as the underlying asset. Rights to his royalties were securitised into ten-year bonds issued at $1000 each. The bondholders were entitled to a share in the royalties on these albums for ten years, after which the bonds matured, the principal was repaid and the royalties returned to Bowie. The approach has been used by a number of other artists since.

Use of IP as collateral with licence back

In this approach, the lending institution takes a charge over the IP which is used as collateral for a loan. The IP is licensed back to the company exclusively. The bank has control over the IP and so is in a strong position should the company require restructuring. Several case studies are reported in the UK's WIPO report, two of which are summarised below.

Eseye

Eseye is an IT company working in cellular networking interoperability, whose founders were serial entrepreneurs having previously founded and sold the company that developed the Zigbee near-field communication standard. The company's IP assets included 19 patent families and a number of national and international trade marks. Eseye raised £4 million in venture debt financing through Virgin Money, facilitated by IP valuation. The money raised put Eseye in a position to achieve the growth needed to close a new equity raise, worth £15 million. The company value appreciated considerably between its equity rounds, enabling it to reinvest more in the business with less dilution.

Inspiretec

Inspiretech is a software company licensing its product into the leisure industry. Its revenues stem from a core base of recurring revenues from ongoing software licences to its platform supplemented by customisation and bespoke development work. The company worked with Lombard who took an ownership interest in the software platform, licensing it back to Inspiretec exclusively. This approach freed up an initial £2.5 million that was primarily used for debt restructuring.

Insurance-backed loans using the IP as collateral

A further approach is emerging particularly in the United States, in which the financing company makes a loan to the borrowing company and this loan, in turn, is covered by an insurance policy, paid for by the borrower, but for the benefit of the finance company, and designed to pay off the loan if the borrower defaults. Using the borrower's IP assets as collateral means the lender will be able to leverage the value of the IP in a restructure, refinance or other scenarios in the event of non-recovery. The cost of the insurance as a one-off premium, which is typically included in the loan along with other costs, such as those for legal, advisers and underwriting.

Example products in the UK

NatWest high-growth IP loan

This product offers loans of £250,000 to £10 million, using IP assets as collateral. It involves NatWest taking a fixed and floating charge over the company's IP assets at a maximum of 50 percent loan to value. Consequently, IP-backed funding from NatWest is only available for businesses with an IP valuation of £500,000 or more. The IP assets are monitored throughout the life of the loan with a full revaluation performed annually, so NatWest can consider growth or impairment. If the IP value goes up after revaluation, it may give the lending business an opportunity to take on more debt. Current fees associated with the Natwest IP-based loan include: a 1 percent set-up fee; a 0.4 percent annual revaluation fee and an interest rate of 3-4 percent over base rate.

HSBC growth-lending, IP-based loan

Launched in July 2022, this loan product is backed by a £250 million (rising to £350 million) fund directed at start-ups. But, like similar funds, the company must have already raised significant equity. In this case, the company must have already raised a minimum of £25 million and have a proven business model and sales track record with more than 20 percent growth over the last two years.

Virgin growth finance

This is a venture debt product offered to IP-rich, high-growth companies with a growing annual recurring revenue of over £2 million which already have a strong professional equity backing and, of course, backed by IP or other proprietary technology. However, the borrower company does not need to be profitable or cash generative at the point of borrowing.

In summary, it is clear that a level of funding is now available to address the finance gap experienced by companies that are IP rich, but tangible-asset poor, looking for non-diluting funding to finance the needs after start-up for scaling the business. However, the criteria for consideration illustrate that these products are aimed at quite late-stage companies with significant IP that is clearly able to support the loan. Earlier stage companies with higher risk remain the domain of less risk averse providers, such as venture capital and business angels.

Matthew Rodgers has long experience with early-stage tech ventures. He is currently a patent attorney at Stratagem IPM in Cambridge, mainly advising start-ups and spin-outs in life sciences. He was previously at BTG and Boston Scientific where he managed the IP in early-stage technologies. He trained as a patent attorney at Bayer CropScience and was previously a research scientist at Rhone Poulanc.

Notes

[1] *Using Intellectual Property To Access Growth Funding*, a report by the British Business Bank, 2018, available at: british-business-bank.co.uk
[2] 'Country Perspectives: The UK's journey', *Unlocking IP-backed Financing*, a WIPO series, 2023, available at: wipo.int
[3] *ScaleUp Annual Review: Scaling Beyond Frontiers*, ScaleUp Institute, 2022, available at: scaleupinstitute.org.uk
[4] Available from the International Valuation Standards Council at ivsc.org.
[5] *Intangible Asset Finance: Moving intangible asset finance from the margins to the mainstream*, WIPO, 2022
[6] 'Country Perspectives: The UK's journey', *Unlocking IP-backed Financing*, a WIPO series, 2023, available at: wipo.int

11

IP STRATEGIES FOR THE SECOND FUNDING ROUND

As you scale, investors are looking at more than the potential of your IP, says Mathias Karlhuber. They now want to know whether it can support future growth and withstand any attacks

In later rounds of funding, investors will closely review how well your intellectual property can support your future growth and how vulnerable it might become to attack. Following an investment, as you gain a higher profile and make more of an impact, your portfolio and your fortitude will be tested not just by your competitors, but by a variety of non-practising entities (NPEs) who own the IP without offering any products or services.

As a start-up, your challenge was to build a decent portfolio of IP in the first place. Once growth is established, you can lose sight of your IP strategy in the long term. As a scale-up, you may focus on maximising the potential of what you already have. The motivation and resources for making constant adjustments to your IP strategy are more limited. As a result, your IP might be coming to the end of its life, giving competitors a chance to enter the market.

It's a scenario to which investors are particularly sensitive. They will expect to see an active strategy in place for securing future revenues. They will also be looking at your ability to defend yourself.

A convincing strategy will depend on your appreciation of the distinctive nature of the protection that IP gives you. You only have a negative right of prohibition, ie, as the owner, you can stop others using your creation, such as a patented invention. However, you do not have a positive right to use it.

So if a product infringes someone else's patents, your marketing can be prohibited, even by someone who isn't an active competitor in your market, so jeopardising an entire investment. So, even if you have a sizeable portfolio, you are not insulated from attacks on your IP.

Investors realise that you can't just map an IP portfolio to your own products and services. It will fall too short in properly accounting for the IP risks. Instead, they will take a close look at the competing IP that surrounds you, as well as identifying others with a stake in technology. Only then, can they take a view of how well you can defend yourself and how prone your industry is to litigation.

So what IP will it take to complete a second funding round? Typically, you will know what could threaten you; you will know the value of your IP to your competitors; and you can anticipate where future competition might lie.

Know what IP is out there

Irrespective of what kind of attack scenario the company might be facing, an obvious prerequisite to a sensible IP risk assessment strategy is to obtain comprehensive knowledge about the IP rights that exist and could potentially represent a risk for your future commercial activities. In the field of patents this knowledge is typically obtained by running a database search that provides information about existing patent applications and granted patents. The hits provided according to the search profile chosen then have to be assessed for their relevance to your current and future products and services.

Such a database search is only a snapshot of the situation at the time it was made and has a blind spot of about 18 months due to the delayed publication of patent applications after filing. Hence, running the search again towards the end of the process is recommended to catch more recently published patents and applications.

The risk assessment itself may become rapidly outdated, as it is based on assumptions about a company's commercial activities, which can rapidly change, particularly once an investment has been made. So, investors will expect an IP strategy to run a search process and profile, typically as continuous monitoring and risk assessment, where new hits are identified and assessed for their relevance to your current and future business.

Know your defensive value

A further element that investors explore when assessing the IP-related risk of an investment is evaluating the company's resilience against attacks by competitors. Checks are made about whether or not the your IP portfolio covers aspects of the technology which are or will be attractive to competitors in the market. If such a position has been achieved or is even within reach, any competitor risking infringing the company's patents will think twice before attacking for infringement of their patents. A prerequisite to this preventive effect is of course that a competitor holding critical patents is itself interested in using the technology covered by the company's patents and is therefore willing to enter negotiations. Hence, under this defensive aspect, the relevance of the company's patents to their own products is less important. Rather, the primary value of your IP portfolio lies in its relevance to existing and future products of the competition.

Technological development and progress in many cases is key to a successful product or service and should be closely covered by your IP portfolio. Nevertheless, a crucial question to be asked when it comes to sensible IP coverage is what will actually sell the product or service. This may not always be the technologically most advanced feature, but might be a side aspect instead, often adding other technologies. Well-known current examples are connectivity features and data collection or processing features that secure or even open new revenue streams. Trying to achieve IP protection covering the selling point or the revenue stream of a product or service may often be way more valuable than protecting the technologically most advanced solution. Such an approach may, of course, significantly increase the defensive value of an IP portfolio.

This strategy may even help revitalise or maintain a dominant IP position that is at risk due to the expiry of the IP covering the basic technology. The combination of an existing technology, for example, a medical device for treating a specific condition with other technologies, such as connectivity, data collecting and processing or data security may provide a competitive advantage that considerably prolongs the success of an existing product. While such approaches are, of course, ubiquitous and become harder to be protected, trying to obtain such protection may be well worth the effort.

Investors expect an IP strategy to set up a filing and prosecution strategy that does not only focus on its own products but keeps the defensive value of patents in mind. Optimally, your company already has a corresponding charting process in place which analyses competitor products against the company's patents and its applications.

Your future competitors

Investors further appreciate finding that a company has implemented an active approach to mitigate IP risks associated with competitor patents. This can happen, for example, by trying to prevent potentially critical competitor patents from being granted or by attacking such a granted patents.

In essence, most of the existing national or regional patent systems provide two ways of attacking patent applications and patents. Depending on the respective national or regional provisions, an attempt to prevent a patent from being granted can be made by submitting a third-party observation or, where applicable, by filing a pre-grant opposition. Challenging a granted patent can either be achieved by filing a post-grant opposition or by other invalidation attacks, such as nullity actions.

It should be noted that, in certain fields of technology or markets, it is customary preventive practice to file such attacks against competitor patents using typically fairly inexpensive opposition procedures, even without the relevant patent being an immediate commercial threat. Such an approach can show considerable commercial foresight.

In the case of NPEs, the only way to offset risks from them is to attack their patents, as they are not susceptible to infringement counterclaims. Some NPEs, rather than developing their own patents, successively acquire interesting patent applications or patents from practising entities to enforce them. It often happens where operators pull out of a field of technology and monetise their related IP by selling it or spinning it off into a licensing entity. Hence, what may once have been the patent of a competitor perceived as less aggressive in the market may well end up in the hands of a considerably more aggressive NPE, the business model of which is to license and, if need be, enforce their patents. For investors, your strategy should take this risk into account.

Licensing agreements with IP holders are another form of risk management. A special licensing scenario may arise with patent pools, where owners combine to license their pooled patents together. Such a scenario is often encountered in the context of standard essential patents which are inevitably infringed if a certain industry standard is to be met. Such SEPs cannot be freely enforced by their owners but are subject to a licensing offer under Frand conditions (fair, reasonable and non-discriminatory). Enforcement is only available if the potential licensee refuses to take a license under these Frand terms. While these patents can be attacked in the same way, the sheer number of them does not lend itself to such an approach. If you have established your exposure and identified the licences you require, investors will take it as a sign that you have a reasonably sophisticated IP strategy.

In summary, as assessing the IP-related risks in a technology company is a comprehensive task for the investor, a company seeking new funding should be prepared to answer a series of questions that provide the investor with a good initial idea of these IP-related risks involved with the investment, as well as if and how these have been approached by the company in the past. If you have replies to these questions to hand, it can greatly simplify the IP-risk assessment process and negotiations with investors.

Mathias Karlhuber is a partner at Cohausz & Florack, a multidisciplinary law firm in Düsseldorf and Munich that supports its clients in all matters relating to IP and unfair competition. He is an expert in technical IP rights in the fields of electronic program guides, medical devices, semiconductor lithography systems, railway technology, vehicle dynamics, crash safety and aerodynamics, specialising as well in data security, micromechanics and general mechanical engineering. He is also active at the IP commission of the International Chamber of Commerce and was its rapporteur on patents for many years. Further details at: cohausz-florack.de.

12

FREEDOM TO OPERATE

Freedom to operate is becoming as integral to creating and growing your innovation as any other form of IP, say Christian Heubeck and Stefan Jellbauer at Weickmann

After a pause during the pandemic, freedom to operate is re-defining itself as a frontline discipline within innovation. Once it might have been enough to have had an idea, claim the intellectual property, then check that you had a path to market.

During lockdown, those rules were suspended. The priority was to find treatments for patients. Legal complications could wait until later.

Now the innovation cycle is back to normal with a new sense of competitive intensity. The speed of what collaborations can achieve under pressure is now accepted. Breakthrough technologies, such as immunology, are being absorbed. Automation is opening up technology landscapes for everyone. Fields, such as personalised medicine, are following the same pattern as smartphones and embedding numerous technologies in one product.

So it is making less and less sense to develop an innovation without knowing to what extent it might depend on someone else's IP. You will soon find it worthless, if a competitor decides to block you and chase you from the market.

So an FTO analysis is becoming as significant as the original IP itself in bringing innovation to market. You have to know where you stand, both for yourself, as well as any potential investors or partners.

In the early stage, as an innovator, you will ask broad questions about mapping technology landscapes to evaluate whether you have found a niche and are heading in the right direction. Later more detailed questions will follow about whether you are in danger of straying too close to someone else's patents and whether you can design around them.

Venture capitalists will also review the strengths of your competitive position before committing any funds and direct investors, notably the Chinese, who might once have been happy to launch in Europe and wait for a reaction, are now undertaking FTOs in advance of market entry.

FTO decisions

Ideally, a founder or an investor will be looking for three to four pages summarising the competitive risks to their IP. Their priority is to make the right business decision, not immerse themselves in the detail of competing IP.

If, instead of an external FTO analysis, they ask the question themselves, they can find themselves swamped with data. Artificial intelligence is now bringing multiple sources within reach of everyone, often with accompanying analysis and visuals. However, it is another matter to reliably interpret such data.

When taking a decision, most ventures prefer to rely on external expertise in filtering hundreds of documents into a short summary of the risks. Unlike AI, such professionals are liable for the recommendations they make.

In their analysis, it is rare that they will find a showstopper that brings a deal to an abrupt halt. Instead, they will highlight competitive risks within the landscape. Once these are established, action can be taken either to design a way round a competitor's IP, negotiate a licence for its use, nullify it or acquire it.

Your competitors, of course, are aware that such steps might be taken to soften their IP. So their claims are now starting to be written in a way that is AI proof, so letting them operate out of your sight, until you have unwittingly launched.

Your ability to avoid such traps, gain from your FTO and put yourself in a position to charge a premium for your IP will depend on:

- how you conduct your search;

- how any rival IP is interpreted;

- what tolerance you have for risk;

- and how well you patrol the landscape in which you operate

Searches, parameters and clusters

At an early stage, a search might include a wide spread of literature, not just patents, as you make an initial evaluation of what direction an innovation could take. As you progress, your search will focus more tightly on patents, assessing the degree to which you are infringing on anyone else's rights.

You will set parameters either by your technology's classification, by your likely competitors or by the territories in which you operate. You are likely to discover hundreds, if not thousands, of potentially relevant patents. So you will probably review the first 50 and then refine your parameters further.

Up until recently, visual representations of patterns and interconnections between these patents weren't generally available. Now you can see a representation of the points at which a technology is clustering, which gives you a focus for which direction to take.

Confidence and gaps

You can spend as much as you like on an FTO. However, during an analysis, you will be trying to bring the initial trawl of potentially hundreds of documents into a set of relevant results within a reasonable schedule and budget.

What happens then depends on your degree of confidence. If you are comfortable with being 80 percent sure, an FTO can happen at speed. At 100 percent, it will take longer and is unlikely to give you a total certainty in any case. Apart from any defects in the system you are searching, you will inevitably encounter a publications gap.

A patent only appears 18 months after it has been filed. So no one can see them before then. For a fast-moving technology, it might be relevant, although it will probably be relying more on trade secrets and first mover advantage. For medical products, the lead times are so long that you can update yourself nearer to launch.

Claim interpretation

Definitions in your competitors' IP bear close scrutiny: in particular, are terms being used consistently? We have just had a case, for instance, in which a patent owner was interpreting a claim in one way for the examiner and in another for validity. Such ambiguity will undermine their IP, opening the way for you.

Because innovation now relies on a combination of so many technologies in one product, it's unlikely that you will rely on one FTO expert. To get down into the underlying technology of personalised medicine, for instance, you will make want to make sure your analysis covers the relative strengths and weaknesses of both your competitor's biochemistry and its AI software.

Find your safe harbour

As an innovative venture, you may end up undertaking one overarching FTO, probably when you start trying to win over investors. It'll be an intense experience.

Or you can anticipate some of the hostile questions that are going to be asked. If you put the right parameters in place and see what risks are coming, your FTO can then become as integral to creating and growing your innovation as any other form of IP.

So let us leave you with an example of a question we are regularly asked. 'At the trial stage, do we have the freedom to use someone else's patented technology, when we won't be including it in our final product?'

Under qualified exemptions in the United States and Europe, the so-called 'safe harbours', the answer is a qualified yes, depending on where you are and what you are doing. Depending on how you resolve the question, you can speed up the commercialisation of your idea. Or you can store up trouble for later.

If you add all such freedoms to operate together as you progress, you will create a series of small, but significant wins in how you perform and how you position yourself competitively. Together, these will add up to a powerful statement when potential investors or potential partners start asking awkward questions about your freedom to operate.

Christian Heubeck and **Stefan Jellbauer** are involved in conducting FTO analyses at each stage of the innovation lifecycle from technology landscaping for start-ups to the interpretation of patent claims for venture capitalists. They are partners at one of Germany's leading IP practices, **Weickmann**, where they work with a mix of research bodies, innovative ventures and the leading IP players. Further details at: www.weickmann.de.

13

CLAIM INTERPRETATION

Ready for legal scrutiny? Variations in how claims are interpreted within the European and German systems will put your patent to the test, say Friedrich Emmerling and Rolf Lechner at BPDE

The number of patent applications submitted to the European Patent Office has been on a consistent upward trend. In 2023, the number of patent applications at the EPO increased by 2.9 percent. This growth reflects an acceleration in innovation, particularly in the domains of digital and green transformation. The digital communication sector has experienced a notable surge in patent activity with an 8.6 percent increase in 2023. The value of patents remains undiminished in safeguarding positions in tomorrow's market.

Further statistics show that the grant rate of patents rose from 61.5 percent to 71 percent between 2015 and 2021. At the same time, however, it is reported that a significant number of patents are partially or completely revoked in opposition appeal proceedings, mostly due to prior art that would have been available or was interpreted and thus assessed differently.[1]

These figures were gathered in the context of ongoing discourse surrounding patent quality, which is pivotal to the system, as the value of a patent depends on its capacity to be enforced. Only when it is capable of withstanding legal scrutiny, particularly in the context of opposition or nullity proceedings, will it be a high-quality patent.[2] This legal scrutiny rests heavily on claim interpretation for defining the subject-matter for testing validity and the scope of protection for determining infringement.

All the same, but different: German and European approaches to claim interpretation

In accordance with German case law, the interpretation of a patent claim is essentially a matter of legal application and always has to be conducted. In the German dual system, claim interpretation is a key aspect to be considered carefully, as it can be tempting to apply a broad interpretation in an infringement proceeding and a narrow interpretation in a validation proceeding. However, it is important to resist this temptation as the Federal Court of Justice (FCJ or *Bundesgerichtshof*) will bring both interpretations into harmony when they come together in the last instance.

Still, practice shows that it still happens: these diverging interpretations are even given a name, the Angora cat phenomenon:

> When validity is challenged, the patentee says his patent
> is very small: the cat with its fur smoothed down, cuddly

and sleepy. But when the patentee goes on the attack, the fur bristles, the cat is twice the size with teeth bared and eyes ablaze.[3]

In infringement proceedings, the scope of protection must be interpreted as broadly as necessary to prove the case. Conversely, in validity proceedings, the subject matter of protection is drawn as narrowly as possible to distinguish the matter for which protection is sought from the prior art. These different points of view are further encouraged by the delayed conduct of nullity proceedings, also known as the injunction gap. But it is not just the system; sometimes these differences in claim interpretation arise in teams which do not communicate enough before writing their submissions.

In recent German case law, it has been repeatedly shown that the FCJ could still overturn the case when both proceedings are brought before it. Notable examples, in which the interpretation was overturned in a decisive manner, are known in German case law under the following keywords: *Gelenkanordnung, Okklusionsvorrichtung, Wärmetauscher, Lenkergetriebe, Anhängerkupplung II, Kreuzgestänge.*[4]

In contrast to the German system, the European patent system before the Unified Patent Court generally makes the decision on the infringement and validity of a patent claim in the same chamber. In a brief summary, a main aspect of the UPC is that the counterclaim pertaining to the same patent in question is admissible before the respective division. This permits both infringement and validity to be adjudicated in a single proceeding. In essence, the same judges will interpret the claims concurrently.

Independent of the infringement proceedings before the national German courts or the UPC, it is possible to file an opposition within nine months of the publication of the grant of a European patent. The opposition procedure is a procedure of legal validity only, which is, however, independent of both the case law of the German FCJ and the case law of the UPC.

The advantage of opposition proceedings is that, in principle, each party bears its own costs and that the patent can be revoked with effect *ex tunc* (retroactively) in all designated contracting states. However, in opposition proceedings, the decision on validity is based on the principles developed by the Enlarged Board of Appeal of the EPO, not according to the respective specific national legal principles of the validation states. So, before filing a patent infringement claim, it is worth assessing whether it is beneficial to wait for the opposition period to have lapsed. It might seem a subtle differences of the developed case law, but requires scrutiny in detail.

Filing an opposition with the EPO results in an even more distinct dual system, as opposition proceedings are distinguished from infringement proceedings, not only in terms of time and personnel, but also in legal terms. In borderline cases, this discrepancy may prove to be a pivotal factor. As we have seen with German case law alone, even a single legal principle can lead to disparate outcomes in the first instances before it is brought together at the FCJ.

The strict formal requirements in opposition proceedings before the EPO is a further difference with nullity actions. It can easily lead to the patent being revoked on basis of added-matter issues that could have been interpreted by the Federal Patent Court (*Bundespatentgericht*) or the FCJ in manner that could survive the nullity action. It is another pitfall to avoid.

This situation is not as bad as it might appear: in litigation, it is essential to make a thorough assessment beforehand, so as not to be surprised. In this respect, it has to be noted that the EPO has the task of applying the European Patent Convention. In the EPC preamble, the participating states agree to strengthen their cooperation in protecting invention through a single procedure for the grant of patents based on standard rules. From the patentee's point of view, a high-quality patent is a legally valid patent, as explained above. It should, therefore, be noted that the EPO should endeavour to create a jurisprudence that enables enforcement.

Hereto, the guiding principles of claim interpretation were clearly defined in G2/88 and G6/88 of the Enlarged Board of Appeal.

> The central role of the claims under the EPC would clearly be undermined if the protection and consequently the rights conferred within individual designated contracting states varied widely as a result of purely national traditions of claim interpretation: and the protocol was added to the EPC as a supplement primarily directed to providing an intermediate method of interpretation of claims of European patents throughout their life, as a compromise between the various national approaches to interpretation and determination of the protection conferred (... so as to combine a fair protection for the patentee with a reasonable degree of certainty for third parties).[5]

However, in contrast to these principles, divergent case law has developed in recent years specifically on the issue of claim interpretation. The current EPO tendency leans towards interpreting the subject-matter of the claim by considering the description and figures to interpret and better understand the wording of the claim if unclarity arises. This divergence is also currently being addressed by a referral to the Enlarged Board of Appeal, G1/24 (heated aerosol). It has to be noted that the UPC and the German FCJ, on the other hand, always interpret the subject matter of the claim by considering the description and the figures in general and apply in this respect the same guiding principle. This practice however would possibly also result in that the description always has to be examined thoroughly as well, which might draw a more intense focus on the content and understanding of the description already made during the examination period. We will see if this aspect will be taken into account in G1/24.

Short overview of recent case law

The relevant case law of the UPC and the FCJ is briefly outlined below. The FCJ can draw on extensive case law on the interpretation of claims. In terms of claim interpretation, the decisions *Polymerschaum I, Spannschraube*, and *Bitratenreduktion*[6] should be emphasised. In summary, it can be said simplistically that German case law uses the description and figures to determine the scope of the claims by applying common sense of the person skilled in the art.

The final judgement of the Court of Appeal of the Unified Patent Court (UPCoA) of 26 February 2024 in *10x Genomics v NanoString* is essentially continuous with the claim interpretation set out in G2/88 of the Enlarged Board of Appeal of the EPO, and states that the guiding principles of Article 69 EPC, defining the extent of protection, are to be applied when assessing the validity according to Articles 52 to 57 EPC of the subject matter of the claims over the prior art:

> This follows from the function of the patent claims, which under the European Patent Convention serve to define the scope of protection of the patent under Article 69 EPC and thus the rights of the patent proprietor in the designated contracting states under Article 64 EPC, taking into account the conditions for patentability under Articles 52 to 57 EPC.[7]

Takeaways

- In consideration of the prevailing practices of the FCJ and the UPC, it is of the utmost importance for the EPO to find and apply equivalent guiding principles on key aspects such as claim interpretation, at least in opposition procedures.

- In practice, it is essential to take into account the arguments presented in the opposition proceedings and in the infringement proceedings respectively. The words used should be wisely selected in both instances, as it will be used for and against you at some point if not at the very end. It is also due to the considerable amount of case law that has developed in the past years a complex and extensive task to assess the benefits for filling an opposition with the EPO versus a nullity action with the FPC.

- The interpretation of the overall claim is a pivotal aspect of any patent dispute procedure. The codified underlying wording of novelty and inventive step is identical in form, yet significant differences may emerge due to the case law that has developed in this regard. It is, therefore, prudent to be aware of and to be able to distinguish between the various approaches in Europe in order to avoid the necessity for complex and lengthy procedures.

Friedrich Emmerling and **Rolf Lechner** at BPDE are at the forefront of enforcing and defending patents in European and German courts, advising clients on the implications of claims interpretation. BDPE has a strong reputation for exceptional work in litigation also involving standard essential patents in the ITC field. Clients rely on BDPE in multiple complex cross-border litigations due to its proven track record. The litigation patent attorneys at BDPE seriously care for clients' business interests in litigation and nullity proceedings, dynamically adopting proposals to find the respective best solution.

Notes

[1] Beat Weibel, 'Patentqualität – cui bono?, *GRUR Patent*, 2023, 133; Daniel X Thomas: 'IPQC meets Uni Osnabruck', blog.ipappify.de, accessed on 10 December 2024; and Daniel X Thomas, 'EPO quality dashboard and corresponding KPI', blog.ipappify.de, accessed on 10 December 2024.
[2] Ann: 'Patentqualität – was ist das, und warum ist Patentqualität auch für Anmelder wichtig?', *GRUR*. 2018, 1114
[3] *European Central Bank v Document Security Systems Inc*, EWCA Civ 192 (Jacob LJ), 2008
[4] BGH, 04.2010 - Xa ZR 36/08, Gelenkanordnung; BGH, 10.05.2011 – X ZR 16/09, Okklusionsvorrichtung; BGH, 10.05.2016 – X ZR 114/13, Wärmetauscher; BGH, 24.09.2019 – X ZR

62/17, Lenkergetriebe; BGH, 02.02.2021 – X ZR 170/18, Anhängerkupplung II; BGH, 02.06.2015 – X ZR 103/13, Kreuzgestänge.

[5.] EPA G2/88, Rn. 4

[6.] BGHm *GRUR*, 2012, 1124 Rn. 27, Polymerschaum I; BGH, *GRUR*, 2015, 1095 Rn. 13, Bitratenreduktion; BGH, *GRUR*, 1999, 909 (911), Spannschraube.

[7.] Anordnung des Berufungsgerichts des EPG vom EPG, 26 Februar 2024, UPC_CoA_335/2023, *GRUR*, 2024, 527

14

LIVING WITH EUROPE'S NEW UNIFIED PATENT COURT

Split proceedings? Bundled cases? Confidentiality? Forum shopping? Jens Pilger at DHS reviews how Europe's Unified Patent Court is shaping up and how life is changing for patent owners

The European patent reform package is based on two pillars, namely the Unified Patent Court (UPC) and the unitary patent (UP), and is potentially the most important new development in the European patent system in the last 50 years (ie, since the European Patent Office itself was established). Starting in the early 1960s, long before the formation of the European Union, there had already been efforts to establish a (unified) European patent system, the most notable result so far being the EPO.

On the one hand, there had been high expectations regarding the new patent court, including bundling all patent infringement proceedings with respect to one European patent in a single trial, making proceedings more efficient, speeding them up and lowering costs. On the other hand, there had been doubts that a common court for so many different EU states could in fact be established and work efficiently. Further, the patent community remained cautious since no one could know how friendly towards claimants or defendants the new court would be in deciding cases.

Finally, on 1 June 2023, the UPC and the UP entered into force. We can now start to draw some conclusions from these first experiences and take a closer look at the first available court decisions. Such familiarity with how the system is evolving may provide tactical advantages for how patent cases are now handled in Europe.

Review of the present architecture

In its present form, the patent reform package has a juridically unique structure, which reflects the challenges in its creation. The UP is in fact a European patent with unitary effect (EPUE), enhancing cooperation between the 18 participating states, not the whole EU. Essentially, the two relevant EU regulations contain no material patent law, but transfer it to an international treaty, the Unitary Patent Court Convention. Although formed by EU law, it is independent of it. No doubt, the exact form that its relationship takes with the EU and the EPO will be put to the test.

The UPC entered into force on 1 June 2023 and, at the time being, 18 member states of the EU take part, while a further six EU member states are at least considering to ratify the UPCC. It should be kept in mind, however, that the 18 current UPC states already represent the third largest economy in the world.

The UPC comprises two central divisions (Paris and Munich) for handling patent infringement and revocation proceedings, as well as separate revocations. Further, the UPC comprises a plurality of local and regional divisions for handling patent infringement and revocation proceedings (in Germany, for example, in Munich, Düsseldorf, Mannheim and Hamburg). The central, local and regional divisions represent the courts of first instance, while the UPC's court of appeal in Luxembourg will represent the court of second instance.

For the classical European patent, proceedings can take place either before the national courts (one or more national trials) or before the UPC (one trial, but only for those national parts, where the corresponding EU member state takes part in the UPC), depending on where the action is filed in the first place. The strategic significance is that it is possible to deny the competence of the UPC to a European patent (a so-called 'opt-out'), for at least seven years, maybe more. It should be kept in mind, however, that the UPC is exclusively competent for unitary patents (and here no opt-out is possible).

Available UPC statistics

The UPC is organised by its registry in Luxembourg from where it runs a case management system (CMS). In the beginning, a high number of opt-out requests were filed (ie, to remove European patents from the UPC system, in particular to avoid central nullity proceedings) and many European patent attorneys had to register themselves as UPC representatives. The UPC's IT system had a difficult start and crashed many times. A few important infringement proceedings even had to be filed using a USB stick, since the CMS did not work in a stable manner.

In the end, however, the registration of UPC representatives worked well and around 500,000 European patents opted out (actually less than expected). The number of pending actions for isolated revocations at the UPC is surprisingly small so far, only around 25. It raises questions about whether fears about the opt-out were too high or whether all relevant patents had opted out.

The dominating language at the UPC at the moment is German, especially since many actions were prepared in German due to unclear language regulations. A shift to English as the dominant language is nevertheless expected. The dominant court seems to be the local division in Munich, having at the time being 36 pending infringement cases, followed by Düsseldorf, Mannheim and Paris. Currently, the dominant sector is mobile communication, followed by medical technology and consumer goods.

First experiences of the unitary patent

A UP can be requested at the EPO after the publication of the grant in the European Patent Bulletin. The time limit for requesting the UP is still only one month. Before grant, applicants will consider if they are planning to request a UP. One full translation of the patent document is required. Even though a translation into English or German may be preferable, the translation can be in any EU language. It can lead to circumstances where, for example, a translation into Spanish can be filed, even though Spain is not yet part of the UPC. In case a validation of a European patent in Spain is planned anyway, and since Spain requires a full translation, it can be a straightforward measure to use the same translation for requesting the UP and for validating the EP in Spain.

In my experience, requests for UPs have been working fine. A frequent question is about machine translations. Even though the translation has only an informative character, I would recommend a human translation, because the UPC may deny a machine one, especially in case of any inconsistencies.

A UP may be especially advantageous when covering a plurality of countries (eg, four or more) and will be kept in force for most or all of them. The UP could be used in infringement proceedings in up to 18 states at the same time with only one trial. It may be seen as a drawback that a UP can be attacked and eventually revoked in one single trial. Further, the number of states cannot be reduced in order to save costs (it is all or none of the 18 states).

First decisions of the UPC

The first decisions of the UPC are becoming available, in particular with respect to preliminary injunctions. These decisions are subject to intensive discussions among those seeking to gain familiarity with how the UPC is going to work.

Confidentiality

The UPC has a wide competency to request proves, many of them relating to sensitive data. In *Avago v Tesla*, an infringement case before the local division in Hamburg, the UPC made a ruling about a confidentiality agreement. It decided that information about the technical implementation of the infringing form and the purchasing prices of chips are confidential information / trade secrets, which are not for public disclosure. The measure, when requesting confidentiality, is 'sufficient certainty'. Since such early cases before the UPC are so intensively observed, it may be advisable to request confidential treatment of sensitive information.

Urgent actions

In *myStromer v Revolt*, a PI was filed by myStromer at the local division in Düsseldorf, referring to a European patent for the frame of an e-bike. Infringement and validity of the patent were considered secured in the required scope, so that the PI was granted without hearing the parties. The PI referred to an upcoming bicycle fair, so its urgency was also accepted. It is reported that the PI was granted within hours, showing a potentially friendly attitude towards patent owners by the UPC. Even after receiving the PI, Revolt continued its display at the fair and on the internet for two hours, as well as exhibiting an infringing bike once again three months after receiving the PI. The penalty it was required to pay was €26,500. As both myStromer and Revolt are relatively small, we can assume that higher penalties will apply to larger companies. From this case, when a PI was urgently required, it appears that the UPC may act quickly, efficiently and in a way that is friendly to patent owners.

Split proceedings

In *Edwards v Meril,* an interim decision was made about which is the same party, which is relevant to the separation of proceedings. Edwards sued Meril India for patent infringement at the local division in Munich. Meril filed in turn an isolated revocation action at the central division in Paris via its Italian group company. The questions arose, if these two cases had to be bundled, since Meril India and Meril Italy should be the same party. Yet, the central division in Paris decided that these groups are not the same party, so that two separate processes are now possible: infringement proceedings in Munich and revocation proceedings in Paris. Munich may now decide to transfer validity or even the whole case to Paris. Alternatively, a stay of the infringement proceedings may be suitable. The UPC enables interesting options for splitting proceedings of a case, separating infringement and revocation, when different parties are involved.

Central and local

In *Amgen v Sanofi*, Sanofi filed an isolated revocation action at the central division in Munich, while Amgen filed an infringement action at the local division in Munich on the same day. The UPC clarified that the time difference (even on the same day) matters, although the infringement action is preferred. In the meantime, another company, Regeneron, filed a revocation counterclaim at the local division in Munich. Regeneron and Sanofi share the same interest but are not the same party. The question is now whether there can be two independent revocation proceedings. From this case, a trend towards a split in proceedings seems to arise. It will be important to observe how the UPC will handle these developments in future, so that proceedings can be planned accordingly. Local divisions may decide to transfer the question of validity to the central division or even the whole case (if the parties agree).

UPC reasoning

In *10x Genomics v Nanostring*, the first decision by the UPC's court of appeals or its court of second instance, a ruling was given on granting a PI. More widely, however, it gave a first detailed insight into the UPC's reasoning. 10x Genomics had filed a preliminary injunction action at the local division in Munich. In contrast to *myStromer v Revolt*, the decision on the patent's validity was not straightforward. *Inter partes* oral proceedings were held and the UPC discussed the relevant points of patentability, essentially applying the practice of the EPO. Munich's local division confirmed that the measure for validity in PI proceedings is 'sufficient certainty', which is in line with the CJEU (Court of Justice of the EU). Based on this reasoning, the PI has been granted in this case.

The UPC's court of appeals agreed with the reasoning of Munich's local division. However, it concluded that the probability of revocation is higher than of maintenance, so that no PI was granted in the end. This case confirms that the UPC can be considered fast, efficient, and friendly to patent owners, especially regarding grant of PIs, even though the court of appeals interpreted the probability of revocation in this case differently than the local division.

In summary, these first decisions show that the UPC works highly efficiently and is friendly towards patent owners. Even though the UPC was established for bundling European patent cases, there seems to arise a trend to splitting proceedings between UPC divisions, provoked by actions of different parties.

Outlook

Further full decisions of the UPC are expected soon, not only regarding PIs. Interest will focus on the question of whether different UPC local and central divisions will apply different reasonings or if a common consensus will be found soon. Depending on these decisions, there may or may not arise an intensive forum shopping. Further, it will be interesting, if the splitting of proceedings will be established or if a trend will arise in the UPC to bundle related cases, even including not the same parties. Based on these developments, tactical decisions may be taken to choose one suitable UPC division or split proceedings between two or even more UPC divisions.

Three new EU regulations are on the way that will also affect the UPC. These regulations concern highly relevant topics such as standard-essential patents (SEPs), compulsory licences and supplementary protection certificates (SPC). To include them within the EU system, it is proposed that they are handled by EUIPO, the EU's IP office, which so far has been responsible for trade marks and designs. It will be interesting to see how these EU regulations will be finally formulated and how they will complement the UPC.

Originally, there were three central divisions. London was removed after Brexit, leaving only Paris and Munich. A third, mainly relating to pharmacy, is being added in Milan. Last but not least, Ireland plans to organise a referendum and may, depending on the outcome, become the 19th UPC state.

Takeaways for patent owners

For patent owners, so far, the following conclusions can be drawn about living with the UPC and the UP in the European patent system:

- The new system does not replace but complements the existing European patent system, adding some interesting options.

- The first decisions of the UPC (mainly regarding PIs) seem to be friendly towards patent owners.

- The standard for evaluating validity of a patent seems to be only 'sufficient certainty'.

- A trend towards a split in proceedings between divisions will encourage some forum shopping.

Dr Jens Pilger, LLM is a German patent attorney and professional representative before the European Patent Office. He is partner at the IP firm DHS in Munich and specialises in patent prosecution, especially in the fields of mechanics, chemistry, electronics, and computer-implemented inventions. For further information: pilger@dhs-patent.de

Appendix

THE HIGH-GROWTH TECHNOLOGY BUSINESS INITIATIVE

Small and medium-sized enterprises or start-ups with the potential for rapid and substantial value creation due to the innovative and scalable nature of their technology-based products or services are typical high-growth technology businesses. Their portfolio of intellectual assets, secured by intellectual property rights, can be pivotal in ensuring a profitable return on their creativity and investments. Building a strong IP portfolio strategically and from the outset may contribute to high growth in various ways, namely by securing market access, facilitating collaborations, strengthening negotiation position, attracting investments or enabling business transactions. However, it is particularly common for early-stage ventures but also for established SMEs to underestimate the significance of IP as they focus on launching products and services.

Having a solid IP strategy and implementing a business-focused IP management system should therefore be in the focus for tech ventures aiming at high growth. Especially in view of the recent introduction of the unitary patent in Europe, which invites businesses to re-evaluate their IP strategies, access to IP and business-related know-how and advice will be even more crucial for decision-makers to achieve their ambitious goals.

The European Patent Office and the Licensing Executives Society International have jointly established the High-growth Technology Business (HTB) Initiative to foster a strategic approach to intellectual property among business decision-makers, train their IP professionals in business-focused IP management practices and support investors in enhancing their knowledge of IP strategy. To achieve those objectives, the HTB initiative provides a wealth of resources available at epo.org/sme, in particular:

- The **HTB forums** are an online event series showcasing success stories of businesses that create value by leveraging their technology through IP. The case studies are presented in a lively presentation-and-discussion format by the chief executive or founder together with an international expert panel and provide the basis for the creation of high-growth technology case studies. The topics centre around areas such as licensing, open innovation, growth financing, build-to-sell, IP strategy and management, as well as digital innovations.

- The **HTB conference** provides participants with a dual track, allowing them to select in break-out sessions their area of focus between business and IP strategy or IP management while being connected by overarching keynote lectures.

- The HTB initiative also pioneered the **HTB clinics** (or IP Business clinics), which offer one-on-one tailored consultations with top experts to business decision-makers or IP professionals free of charge. These experts cover a broad range of areas, including IP strategy, business development, licensing, technology transfer, technology investment, IP transactions, mergers and acquisitions and more.

- **Publications** by experts engaged with the HTB initiative typically build upon and further develop content created for training events, to increase dissemination and impact. They provide practical insight into relevant topics for early-stage and established tech ventures, including technology commercialization, transactions, negotiation, open innovation, IP enforcement and people management.

- **Innovation case studies** comprise technology transfer, SME and high-growth technology case studies. Technology transfer case studies demonstrate how patents enable the transfer of technology from R&D organizations. They depict the process from the initial idea in the laboratory to the introduction of products and services in the market. SME case studies highlight companies that strategically leverage IP for their benefit, offering detailed insights into their practices related to IP management. High-growth technology case studies are audio-visual materials based on recordings form the HTB forums, highlighting the main takeaways.

- **HTB learning** comprises several modules in the e-learning centre of the EPO Academy. The on-demand modules on IP strategy are complemented by synchronous online live sessions allowing group work and support by mentors, facilitating self-paced learning. Similarly, IP management courses are offered.

- The LESI-initiated **HTB business community** on LinkedIn serves as a community platform enabling supporters and members to share content and experience, as well as to network.

The EPO-LESI HTB taskforce invites you to make use of the broad training offers developed to date for the HTB initiative and to follow the HTB community on LinkedIn. This will allow you not only to enhance your own skills and know-how but also to share them with the community, contributing to the improvement of the innovation ecosystem in Europe and beyond.

Further details at epo.org/high-technology-businesses and updates at linkedin.com/company/htbcommunity.

ABBREVIATIONS

AI	Artificial intelligence
CII	Computer-implemented investions
CJEU	Court of Justice of the European Union
CMS	Case management system
CPC	Community Patent Convention
CRO	Contract research organisation
EBITDA	Earnings before interest, tax, depreciation and amortisation
EIC	European Innovation Council
EISMEA	European Innovation Council and SMEs Executive Agency
EP	European patent
EPC	European Patent Convention
EPUE	European patent with unitary effect
ETSI	European Telecommunications Standard Institute
EUIPO	European Union Intellectual Property Office

Frand	Fair, reasonable and non-discriminatory
4IR	Fourth Industrial Revolution
FCJ	Federal Court of Justice
FDA	Food and Drug Administration (US regulator)
FPC	Federal Patent Court
FTO	Freedom to operate
GDPR	General Data Protection Regulation
HTB	High-growth technology business
IA	Intellectual asset
ICT	Information and communications technologies
IP	Intellectual property
IPC	International patent classification
IPO	Initial public offering
IPR	Intellectual property right
IoT	Internet of things
IVSC	International Valuation Standards Council
ML	Machine learning
MVP	Minimum viable proposition
NDA	Non-disclosure agreement
NFC	Near-field communication
NLP	Natural language processing
NPE	Non-practising entity
PI	Preliminary injunction
R&D	Research and development
SEP	Standard essential patent
SME	Small and medium-sized enterprise
SPC	Supplementary protection certificate

TRL	Technology readiness level
UP	Unitary patent
UPC	Unified Patent Court
UPCA	Unitary Patent Court Agreement
UPCoA	Court of Appeal of the Unified Patent Court
USPTO	United States Patent and Trademark Office
WIPO	World Intellectual Property Organization